Wise Men from the East and from the West

The Religious, Economic and Social Traditions of Eastern and Western Cultures

By Abraham Mitrie Rihbany

PANTIANOS
CLASSICS

Published by Pantianos Classics

ISBN-13: 978-1-78987-264-4

First published in 1922

Contents

Introductory Chapter - A Natural Question v

Part One - East Is East and West Is West 10

Chapter One - The Two Minds 10

Chapter Two - Alien Influences 12

Chapter Three - The Passive Type and the Aggressive Type 17

Chapter Four – The Symbol of Authority 22

Chapter Five - Peace and Freedom 26

Chapter Six - Leaders 30

Part Two - Religious and Social Tendencies in the East and in the West 37

Chapter Seven - What of Religion? 37

Chapter Eight - Man Is Not Incurably Religious 39

Chapter Nine - Holy Books 44

Chapter Ten - The Inner Sphere and the Outer Sphere 48

Chapter Eleven - The Grand Synthesis 50

Chapter Twelve - Industry Plus Life 53

Chapter Thirteen - The Mandate of Business 58

Chapter Fourteen - A "Working" Leisure Class 64

Part Three - Points of Contact between the East and the West 70

Chapter Fifteen - Invasions, Ancient and Modern..................................... 70

Chapter Sixteen - The Results.. 73

Chapter Seventeen - The Revolt of the East against Western
Domination... 80

Chapter Eighteen - The East at the Paris Peace Conference 86

Chapter Nineteen - The French in Syria 97

Chapter Twenty - The Restoration of the Turks to Power 108

Chapter Twenty-One - Zionism A New Eastern Problem..................... 114

Chapter Twenty-Two - The Spirit over the Chaos............................. 124

Introductory Chapter - A Natural Question

BOOKS are fated to be "introduced." Why this is so, fellow craftsmen and many of the reading public know. The custom is old; but, like many other things, the "introduction" has undergone some changes with the passing of time. In earlier days, as a general rule, the introduction constituted a summary of the book. In those good old days the author deemed it necessary to state in the introduction, in swaying Miltonic phraseology, what he was going to say in the body of the book, and then proceed to say it in the "following chapters." In some cases the introduction rendered the book quite dispensable.

In more recent times the character of the introduction has generally been changed. It is now used to present subject-matter which is a little more than kith and a little less than kin to that which the book is intended to contain: such matter as the general subject of the book calls for, but which is not vital enough to form an organic part of the book itself.

Following the current custom, I wish to devote this opening chapter to the consideration of a question which I feel my comparative study of the East and of the West in this volume is likely to raise.

The question seems to me to be a natural, although not always a pertinent, one. The case is not altogether hypothetical. And while the attitude which this question reveals is that of a certain class, yet the interrogation exists potentially in the general consciousness of a people whose life is critically studied by a writer of alien birth.

So far as my own personal experience goes as an Eastern-Westerner, I cannot justly say that I have much cause for complaint. The cordial reception which my former publications have had in this country and in England leads me to believe that in itself alien birth imposes no discredit upon an author's good faith. Yet, even as one of the most highly favored alien-born citizens in this country, I have encountered the question I have in mind, at times in most unexpected quarters. Its tone is only rarely harsh and overbearing. It is often put as any other question which is asked by honest seekers for information. Nevertheless, the very character of the question in its relation to an alien thinker seldom fails, especially at a public meeting, at least to seem to dispute the right of such a person to criticize a social order which extends to him its hospitality.

The form in which this question is put is generally something like this: "Your criticism of Western civilization may, or may not, be correct; in either case, where do you prefer to live, in the East, or in the West?"

The challenge here, though very ingenious, is not hard to see. The question resolves itself into this: "If the defects and faults with which you charge Western civilization are to your mind real, why then are you here? Why do you not depart hence, shaking off the dust from your feet as you go?"

The naturalness of this question is too obvious to be stated at any great length. Let us place it upon the head of that convenient scapegoat known as "human nature." The tendency to question at least the judgment, if not the motive, of an alien critic of a people's life is universal among men. Anglo-Saxon writers who have undertaken to pass judgment upon the life and institutions of alien peoples, among whom they happened to dwell, have had to face similar resentments and have been subjected to like censures as those inflicted by the Anglo-Saxons themselves upon those who criticize their life and institutions. I well remember how in Syria, even before the present restlessness had invaded the minds of men everywhere in the world, the spoken and written comments of English and American missionaries and other writers on the life of our own people were resented by the enlightened natives, who were, in the majority of cases, the pupils of those missionaries.

"Just think of it!" I often heard it said; "we are being scandalously criticized by these foreigners who scarcely know as yet how to speak our language. When will the time come when we shall be able to establish our own educational institutions and get rid of all foreigners?" Such are the failings of human nature in every people under the sun.

But the question before us becomes both natural and pertinent in the case of those Easterners who come to America and England wearing the air of supreme spiritual wisdom: those Easterners who commit themselves to a theory of Western civilization in advance of an accurate knowledge of the life of that civilization, and who pose in those hospitable countries as the compassionate saviors of a lost race. Their idea usually is that the realities of the spiritual life are thickly veiled from Western eyes and that Western peoples are so pitiably deluded as to mistake the mechanics of life for its vitality, and the externals of life for its inward essence.

I am aware of the fact that the position of such self-styled "Eastern seers" does not differ from that of those Anglo-Saxon superiors who style all the Eastern people among whom they happen to be "the poor natives," nor from the position of certain American "reformers" of the native stock who have nothing but condemnation for the land of their birth and residence. Listening to such exponents of human rights and interpreters of American institutions, one, a foreigner especially, if he is easily convinced, is led to believe that this great country has experienced an uncontrollable moral haemorrhage which has sapped its life. He is led to imagine that the ship of state must be on the rocks, although the drunken crew does not fully realize the horror.

But while this is the attitude of some "reformers" of American nativity, nevertheless one wrong judgment does not by any manner of means make another wrong judgment right. If the mistaken foreign critic is willing to be corrected, he may be an asset to the country he criticizes. If, however, he simply claims to speak untruth by a divine right, he should be "handed his passports" and given every possible facility to seek climes more congenial to his soul.

In the case of such critics, I repeat, the question, "If this country is as bad as you say it is, why are you here?" is both natural and pertinent. I would extend the courtesy also to native-born critics of a similar character. The mere accident of birth carries with it no right to such license. A native-born Jonah is even a greater danger to the ship of state than a foreign-born Jonah. The former cannot be so easily suspected, not to know the truth of the statements he makes, as the latter. The rightful place of either and of both is in the belly of the whale, until repentance effects their release.

But in the case of those critics, of whatever nativity, whose good faith and earnest and careful seeking of the facts makes "hem one with the soul of the country they criticize, our question is not pertinent. Anglo-Saxon civilization has profited by the labors of foreign critics, as its own scholarly and humane critics have benefited other peoples. It would be decidedly against the genius of this civilization to suppress within its borders, or exclude from respectful consideration on account of race or language, the social and political judgments passed upon it by any well-intentioned thinker. The dynamics of any true civilization are spiritual, and spiritual gifts are the exclusive possession of no one race or people. They are human assets which every nation should gather into her own treasure-house.

The nobler spirit of the present age wars against assumed and arbitrary exclusiveness. The interrelations of the peoples of the world are inconceivably more extensive and more complex than ever they were before in the history of the world. We are trafficking to-day internationally, not only with goods and finance, but with thought and sympathy. The intermingling of peoples goes on also on a similar scale. Racial bloods, as well as racial thoughts, are being fused together as never before, and the idea of democracy renders the word "foreigner" of uncertain meaning. Today the good spirit "which searcheth the deep things of God" divides mankind, not into foreigners and natives, but into good and bad. He who is of this spirit finds or should find himself an integral unit of civilized society anywhere in the world. The stranger, the foreigner, the alien, is he who holds no kinship with the spirit of truth and good will. It is he whose religious, political, and social theories are subversive of the right principles of orderly and decent human existence, and not he who happens to have been born in another country than that in which he resides. This being the case it logically follows that the moral problems of any country are the problems of civilization in general. As such they should be the chief concern of every beneficent thinker of whatever race. This should apply especially to those of us of foreign birth who have found in this great country a much-coveted home and deeply cherished opportunities.

It is with these thoughts in mind that I approach my present task. I am no longer a foreigner whose views of American life are a mere intellectual formula; no longer a curious observer of an alien civilization whose course and destiny are none of my concern. I could not be such an individual, even if I would. America, vast and undefinable, has entered into my soul. All her waves and her billows have gone over me. I am in this country from deliberate and, I believe, wise preference. Both as a territory and as a human society America is to a newcomer a revolutionary idea. It is a breaker of old ties, a modifier of old notions, a revealer of a new heaven and a new earth. What it has been, what it is, and what it might be as an advancer of civilization, are almost overpowering thoughts. They make a criticism of certain phrases of its life a duty too sacred to be evaded.

To my great admiration for America's fundamental character, I would add my admiration for the Anglo-Saxon race in general. I am not conscious of any antagonism in me toward any other of the great races of the modern world. I simply feel an inward partiality toward this race as one feels drawn toward a person he loves. In early youth, when I first came in touch with Western educational institutions in my native land, I woke up to find myself possessed of this tendency. The Englishman (in those days we generally thought of both the English and Americans in our midst as English) seemed to me to be the embodiment of dignity and integrity. My further acquaintance with the son of this race has not been seriously disappointing. My early conception of him still holds. I admire him to-day as a truth teller, as this world goes, as a champion of freedom within a just law, a lover of home, and as one who has high regard for woman and child. I am also mindful of his faults, chief among which are his haughtiness, his commercialism, and his tendency to believe that he is divinely appointed to exercise authority over "inferior" races. This latter tendency, which is born largely of the commercialistic mind, has been greatly modified in the American Anglo-Saxon, but remains strong in the original stock. And while I think that the noblest members of this race represent the super-type of man on the earth to-day, I am not blind to the fact that the Anglo-Saxon is also capable of serious moral lapses. I do not feel inclined to say unqualifiedly that the good Anglo-Saxon is very good, and the bad Anglo-Saxon is horrid, but I am aware of the fact that, as certain chapters of his history show, this man is capable when he wills of doing a great deal of harm. As a type he is not a breeder of assassins and blood-thirsty anarchists, but he is capable of forcing the opium trade on a great people and of seeking to own the whole earth, if circumstance favored his designs.

In venturing to add my mite in these simple, plebeian observations to the contributions of the writers on such subjects as this, I have not been actuated by much sympathy on my part with the idea that American or Anglo-Saxon civilization in general, is hopelessly on the verge of failure. Such a notion, I am convinced, does not square with the facts. Of course no civilization is ever too great to collapse when the springs of its spiritual life are allowed to dry up. The law of retribution is no respecter of persons, or of races. But I do not think that the constructive forces of Western civilization have become so ineffective as to call only for lamentations and anguish of soul. The threatening danger arises rather from the fact that many of those constructive forces are being slowly but surely diverted into other than their proper channels. The battle, however, has not been lost. It is perfectly possible to change formation and win the day.

Nor is my comparison of the East with the West an invidious one. The vast forward strides which the West has made in modern times on many lines makes it irrational to compare the East with it as a social and political equal. Certainly my purpose is not to press a preconceived theory, regardless of the facts. My aim is rather to think and speak with reference to certain natural endowments which have tended to make the Easterners and the Westerners what they are in their respective spheres, and to venture an opinion as to how these two worlds can, profitably to both of them, form points of spiritual contact with one another. I feel that the sifting and overturning of peoples and nations which the many modern social and political agencies are effecting, and the fearful consequences which the application of brute force to human problems never fails to bring about, require a change of method in the dealing of the West with the East. In one sense what the sword brings the sword takes away. In another sense the sword brings that which it never can take away, and that is, Hatred.

I am fully conscious of the magnitude of the task I have set for myself. I am aware also of the meagerness of my capacity adequately to interpret the tendencies I have chosen to deal with in the following chapters. Nevertheless, I am sending forth this volume as an appeal to better-qualified writers and to the nobler minds among the public in this country and in England to give this subject the wise and sympathetic attention it deserves. The problem is neither political nor sectional. It is human, it is spiritual, and only the wise men from the East and the wise men from the West working together as friends and as spiritual thinkers can effect its proper solution.

Part One - East Is East and West Is West

Chapter One - The Two Minds

THERE is an Oriental mind, and there is an Occidental mind. They are two distinctive types of mind. The twain may meet, but they never can be so joined together that they cannot be put asunder. The difference between them is like the difference between the metals; it is constitutional. Of course, if we contemplate the human mind with reference to its essence, we shall find it to be one and the same in all men. The essence is the realm of undifferentiated possibilities; it is the realm, not of articulate minds, but of general mentality which is common to all intelligent creatures. Yes, "there is one mind common to all individual men." Yet that one mind works differently in an Emerson from what it does in a Turkish customs officer. The seer who spoke this generality must have had reference either to the primitive substance of mind, or to the minds which had full access to the deep secrets of the universe. From the very nature of the case such minds must be alike. Just as in essence all mentality is one, so also, when the supreme good of evolution is reached by man, all minds become one in the glory of self-fulfilment.

But when we consider the human mind as we now know it; when we study it as it has been manifested in the various races, and with regard to its preferences, fixed racial habits, and methods of procedure, we are compelled to admit that there is an Oriental mind which is vitally different in many respects from the Occidental mind. We may be able to understand how such differences have come to be in the process of the centuries; we may be able to see also how they might have been avoided if certain circumstances could have been changed into certain other circumstances. Nevertheless, those differences exist, and, therefore, compel our recognition of them. It is they, as much as the geographical position of those two worlds, which give the East and the West their designations in human speech and their distinctive characteristics.

Speaking in the language of Creation, in the light of my knowledge of both the East and the West, I feel inclined to say that the essential differences which appear between the races of men must have been in the beginning in the mind of the Creator. They could not have been "accidental variations from type." Variation is only the method by which the inherent differences are revealed. I am mindful of the scriptural saying that God "hath made of one blood all nations of men." But I suspect that either the "one blood" does not mean the one mind, or that there must have been a material difference in the *making* of those nations. As in chemical compounds, the ratios in the compositions must have been different, although the basic elements were the same.

But the language of Creation is not very popular in these days of scientific glory. That language is being relegated to the past, whatever that may mean. It is considered to be full of intellectual pitfalls and beset with immovable philosophical difficulties. So I will turn to Evolution, the enchanter of the modern mind.

According to the theory of evolution the Oriental mind remains as Oriental as though it had been created to be so. From the beginning, ever since the tendency toward variation proceeded to manifest itself in guiding the course of human evolution, the Oriental mind as such began to be hammered into shape. The plastic possibilities of its infancy began to unfold under Eastern skies. The climate, the mountains, the hills, the rivers, and the forests of that ancient world distilled the essence of their being into the mentality of the Oriental. The stars from their silent and clear depths in the Eastern firmament shed upon him their sacred influences. They were the first scrolls in which he read the word of God. Day unto day they uttered speech to his listening soul, and night unto night showed knowledge. The contemplation of his own being revealed to him the sublime fact that he was fearfully and wonderfully made. He did not discover the process of his own making; he simply stood facing the mystery of it with reverent awe. His meditations, his prayers, his acts of adoration, streamed out of his soul as responses to the whisperings of the wonders of his Eastern world and fixed the essentials of his character.

Centuries of isolation, geographically and socially, and his contentment with the order of things as it is, have given the Oriental, as it has the other branches of the human race, a character of his own wrought by the labors of countless millenniums.

Yet, even in view of all this, I do not wish to run the risk of being called old-fashioned in this age of all manners of new thought. I do realize that evolution does not mean fixity of character. I do realize that what has been built by a process of evolution can be changed or reconstructed by the same process. Yes, *by the same process.* Nature hates to be forced, and will not be forced. She is hotly jealous for her prerogatives and sternly opposed to a hasty manipulation of her laws. If the wrath of man "worketh not the righteousness of God," it certainly cannot impose its forcible methods upon nature. The patient, centuries-long building of the character of a race, the slow instilling of sentiments and hopes in its soul by natural agencies, and under conditions many of which can never be gathered together again, cannot be supplanted by a hasty human mandate, with a view to reversing the original process and changing the structure of that race's life.

To the East, life on the whole has for many centuries been an inheritance. For many centuries the East has harked back to the "wisdom of the ancients" as the everlasting truth. To the Oriental, the old oracles spoken by holy prophets are the fixed stars which guide the course of his earthly pilgrimage.

To him "seeking" is the search for those perfect and complete truths which were given by Heaven "from the beginning" for the instruction of man. "He that giveth his mind to the law of the Most High, and is occupied in the meditation thereof, will seek out the wisdom of the ancients, and will be occupied in prophecies. He will keep the sayings of men of renown, and where subtle parables are, there will he be also." To the East, life is an inheritance; to the West, an evolution induced by persistent personal effort. The one has been a mystical contemplator of what is, as it has been revealed by the creative power; the other, an inquirer into nature's laws and a dissector of its body. The civilization of the one rests on agriculture and religion; the civilization of the other on industry and education. As a result the Easterner has become the religious teacher of the whole world, and the Westerner its intellectual and political liberator. [1]

In saying there is an Oriental mind and an Occidental mind as two distinctive types of mind, I do not mean that the peoples of the East and the peoples of the West should remain forever alien to one another. My plea is that they should understand one another sympathetically and recognize their fundamental differences as desirable traits which by supplementing one another may work out the problems of civilization. Forcible methods in the attempt to change a people's life can only destroy, but cannot fulfill.

[1] For a fuller account of the differences between the Oriental and the Occidental minds see my book, *The Syrian Christ,* especially Part II, entitled "The Oriental Manner of Speech." (Houghton Mifflin Company, Boston.)

Chapter Two - Alien Influences

IT is, of course, possible to Orientalize an Occidental, and to Occidentalize an Oriental, by permanently transplanting him in early youth to the new environment and thus giving him a new birth and nurture. But you cannot change the fundamental traits of a race by simply subjecting that race to the "influences" of another. For many centuries the East has been invaded by the West and intermittently placed under its domination. In successive waves the "superior culture" of the West has flowed over the more ancient and passive East. The Greeks, the Romans, the Crusaders, and the more recent imperialistic colonizers of Gauls and Saxons have, all of them, sought to awaken the East from its deep slumber and lead it to the fresher springs of their own respective civilizations, but to little purpose. The horse has been led to the water, but could not be made to drink. In the process of the centuries that hoary Orient threw off the thin veneer of alien civilizations as a healthy person throws off a cold, and resumed the even tenor of its way. India, Syria, Egypt, and the other North African countries of to-day will no more effectively yield their souls to their modern "civilizers" than did their predecessors yield their inner being to Greece and Rome.

The Oriental mind cannot be said to be utterly unchangeable. It is flexible and can imitate when it wills. But it seems, during its inconceivably long history, to have tried "all things" and firmly decided to be conservative, or at least not to allow itself to be tossed to and fro by every wind of doctrine that blew from the yet youthful and restless West. Consciously and unconsciously the submission of the East to the West has always been temporary. The soul of that older world has always managed to rid itself of the "superior" tendencies which the newer world sought to infuse into it, and to regain its ancient repose.

Sometime ago a student in a women's college in this country, who had spent many years in Syria, undertook to describe to some of her student friends the broad-tailed Syrian sheep. All went well with her until she stated to her interested hearers that the tail of the Eastern sheep, which is a lump of fat similar in consistency to the camel's hump, weighed in some cases as much as fifty pounds. The incredulity of those students was further intensified when the young woman added that the Easterners attached to the body of the very fat sheep a small cart on which the tail rested, thus enabling the woolly creature, by dragging the little wagon, to walk more comfortably than he otherwise could. The girl stated that she had only heard of the cart, which had been used since the days of the Romans, but that she was absolutely certain about the size and weight of the tail of the sheep, because she had seen many such sheep during her sojourn in the Eastern country. In the absence of tangible evidence and of witnesses, the girl was hilariously jeered at by her incredulous friends and told that she "must have been dreaming." Not willing to be set down as a visionary, the narrator of the strange story wrote imploring me to back her up by writing her a corroborative letter by which to confound her adversaries. I was glad to come to her assistance, not only with the desired letter, but also with a photograph of a large Syrian sheep, which I happened to have. The picture gave indisputable representation of the huge tail .of the sheep, but not of the cart. That vehicle, which I never saw in Syria, I said to her was an ancient Roman device. When the Romans finally left that country, the cart, like everything else that was Roman, went with them, and the Syrian sheep remained in Syria.

However, it may be said here that no one should be so boldly dogmatic as to predict the fixity of the Oriental character forever. The times and conditions have changed since the days of the ancient Greeks and Romans. The influences of those peoples upon the East were very much different from those exerted by the modern Western nations. Experimental science and applied science were only very slightly known to the Greeks and the Romans. Practically they had no machinery in the modern sense of the term. Besides, they were succeeded by the Arabs in the East, who were primitive in their mode of thought and life and hostile to all "idolatrous" institutions. The savage Tartars, also, later swept the East like a devastating flood, leaving nothing behind them which they could destroy. Furthermore, the Greeks, the Romans, and the Crusaders did not enter so deeply into the life of the East as the modern European nations have entered, nor was the East then so eager to borrow from the West as it is to-day. Modern science, modern education, and modern social habits are steadily pouring from the West into the East and deeply penetrating and expanding its life. The modern means of communication, such as the railroad, the automobile, the telegraph and the telephone, all "made in the West," are now in the East. Other products of the modern factory which are being introduced into that part of the world are gradually changing the status of labor and of the ancient, simple native industries.

Western educational institutions in the East are causing revolutionary intellectual changes among the upper and the equally limited middle classes of the people. The Western-educated Easterner is no longer satisfied with his intellectual and social inheritance. He also is becoming increasingly infatuated with the word "progress," and inclined to see an intimate connection between progress and the modern inventions of the West. He wears Western-made and Western fashioned garments, and finds the Western languages more flexible and of richer sources than his native tongue. He sees the Westerner slowly but surely becoming master of the East. With this realization a feeling of inferiority spurs the Easterner to quicken his pace, and, by adopting Western methods, rise to an equality with his Occidental invader.

Another significant factor is the Eastern immigrant in the West. There was a time even within my memory when the West was a mysterious world of untold wonders, which only a few Easterners had the distinction of visiting. The tales which such visitors brought with them from the land of the *afrenj* were much like John the Revelator's description of the New Heavens.

In the last forty years a great host of Orientals have emigrated to Western countries, and the stream is still flowing. These Orientals have found the West a "wonderful world," but not a supernatural world. They have found its denizens to be men and women not much different from themselves. That its achievements are not superhuman, but could be imitated even by the passive East. That while the achievements of the Western nations are great, their problems are great also. The fantastic idealization of the West has lost much of its magic for these Easterners and become more rational. In other words, the more intelligent Eastern immigrants are now convinced that it is not impossible for the East to adopt the desirable features of Western civilization, if not to evolve a similar order of things within its own life. At least we may be certain that those Easterners who have so intimately known the West never will be satisfied with the life of the East as they knew it in their younger days.

These circumstances, then, which did not prevail in the days of the Greeks and the Romans, cannot be set aside as negligible. They are bound to make the influences of the modern West more permanent in the life of the East.

However, before such conclusions can be accepted as valid, two important factors must be considered, especially with reference to the Middle and Near East.

First, the Eastern mind is constitutionally averse to being mechanicalized. The scientific systematizing and standardizing of the various affairs of life is to the Easterner a sort of bondage. To him genius must be free. I very much doubt whether factory labor of the highly specialized Western sort will ever become congenial to him. It is not so very congenial even to the scientific West. The Easterner sees this. The feverish restlessness of the Western peoples and their vexing problems warn the Easterner that an industrial civilization is no royal road to contentment and peace. But I shall come to this in later chapters.

There are to-day industrial establishments in the East, some of which are completely under native control. In my boyhood days French silk spinning factories were established in the East, some of them in the region where I was living. Native operatives flocked into those factories, where they were doomed to toil from twelve to fifteen hours a day for wages ranging anywhere from two cents for children to about fifteen cents for adults per day. The large gains of the French manufacturers lured certain of the native rich to establish such factories themselves. So they did. But in the course of some forty years almost every one of the native manufacturers went to the wall. Native owners, native superintendents, native accountants, and native operatives soon began to chafe under the exactions of "systematic" work. The operators could not rule the operatives with a rod of iron as the French adventurers did, who, clothed with their extraterritorial "rights," lived practically above the law of the land. The early gains of the native manufacturers and the luxuries which those gains induced proved the owners' undoing. Poetry and romance so dear to the Eastern mind, soon reasserted themselves and finally ruined the business. ,

Such misfortunes, however, may be ascribed to the adventures of the inexperienced in business in any country. The entire situation may be changed for the better through wider experience and closer contact with the West. The Easterners may yet become so reconciled to the use of machinery and so strongly attracted by its yield of wealth as to make a success of modern industrial enterprises. This may all be, but I cannot make myself believe it. The Easterners may make good use of machinery "made in the West"; they may acquire steadiness and skill in its use under the guidance of Western experts; but not if they are to manufacture the machinery themselves in any considerable quantities and with *scientific precision.* Successful competition in this field with the West seems to me to be beyond Eastern skill. It is true that so far Japan has demonstrated her ability to do all this, and the far-famed genius of the Chinaman may yet do no less. But as for the rest of the East, the signs are not nearly so promising.

I do not mean in the least to ignore, or even to minimize, the beneficial effects of an industrial system gradually introduced into the East and conducted first of all with a view to human welfare. Yet my opinion is that every lover of humanity should ardently hope that the East may never become so fond of machinery as the West is. At least the sudden introduction of Western industrial methods into the East would, I think, be calamitous. I dread to think of what would become of that ancient world if in the next fifty years the Western factory system were established in it. With the lack of education among the masses, and the absence of a large middle class to act as a shield for the weak and a curb to the strong, the joining of forces by Eastern and Western "promoters" of industrial enterprises in the East, whose purpose is "undreamed-of profits," would mean no less than the reduction of those untutored masses to a worse slavery than prevailed under the pyramid builders.

The East needs an industrial awakening, but this must be brought about very slowly. It must come no faster than a system of education, designed not only to train those masses in the right use of hand and brain, but to awaken them to the fact that they are members of the human family endowed with the inalienable right to life, liberty, and the pursuit of happiness. Let the West in its dealing with the East along these lines take its own misadventures into account. The repetition of such misadventures in the now restless but less intelligent East would create social problems whose solution would baffle the ingenuity of mankind.

Second, the permanence of Western influence in the life of the East will depend upon the character of the final adjustment of the relations between the two worlds. If the end is to be friendly cooperation, which shall guarantee to the East a life of its own, free from Western political domination, then we have reason to hope that the East will remain gladly receptive of Western ideas and eager to adopt Western educational and industrial methods. If however, the Western imperialist means to have his way in the East, the results are bound to be much less gratifying, much less beneficial to either the East or the West. The dull but ominous rumbling which at present invades the hearing of the world indicates unmistakably that the spirit of revolution against the West is agitating the East. And such a cataclysm if it ever comes will certainly sweep out of the East the Westerners and everything Western. Hatred is never constructive. The wise men from the West, who place humanity above its possessions and good will among peoples above monetary gain, must not allow the "market"-seeker to dominate their councils, and, by exploiting the East, sow in the minds of its peoples the seeds of hatred and revolution.

The Easterner can be changed and made an asset to modern civilization when he is surrounded by influences such as we Easterners find in this land of our adoption.

Many of us who were transplanted from the East to the West in early youth have for all practical purposes been Westernized. We have learned to love America and to be loyal to the flag and the Republic for which it stands. We have found in this country in full bloom many things which we only dreamed of and longed for in the Old World. First, we were carried along almost unconsciously by the mighty tide of American life. Later, we began to choose and find our place in this vast social order. Later, still, we began to discover that not everything we brought with us from the East was bad, nor everything we found in the West was good. So far as possible our choice of Western traits became more discriminating with the passing of time. We have found that the fundamentals of the good life are the same in the East as in the West. Now we know that in both these worlds, if a man gain the whole world and lose his own soul, he is damned already. That if a man knows all mysteries and all knowledge and has not love, he is nothing. A virtuous woman in the East is like a virtuous woman in the West. In both these worlds a neighbor is considered to be better than a spy, and a truth-teller better than a liar.

So we finally decided to choose of our old, as well as of our new, heritage whatsoever things are true, honest, just, pure, lovely, and of good report, and to leave, nay, to fight, the rest.

But we have been able to do all this because we have been left free to choose. We have had no alien invader to force us to adopt his ways of living. We have had no colonizer to hold for us the scriptures in one hand and the repeating rifle in the other, and no foreign imperialist seeking in our own land a "sphere of influence," yet looking down upon us as "poor natives." The change which we have experienced from youth to maturity has come upon us as a wooing influence, consequently it has made us love our adopted country, without despising the land of our birth.

The same cannot, of course, be said of those who have been so transplanted in their maturer years. Such persons cannot be so easily, if ever, transformed. The best we can hope for from them is that they may become stepping-stones for the second generation to climb upon to the shining heights: to lay down their lives in the hope that their children may attain that which was impossible for them to reach.

As I shall state more fully in the latter part of this book, if the West disinterestedly desires to spread its superior culture over the East, its means must not be carnal weapons. Truth and love do not need machine guns to make them attractive to the human mind. Their own ineffable charms guarantee for them the victory.

Chapter Three - The Passive Type and the Aggressive Type

ETHNOGRAPHERS tell us that by origin the Occidentals and the Orientals were one. They assert that in the very remote past the more aggressive tribes of Central Asia, the original home of the human race, pushed their conquests westward and planted their colonies from the shores of the Black

Sea to the mountains of Wales, and thus became the ancestors of the Western nations. On the other hand, those tribes and clans which preferred a life of contemplation and submission to vision and dream remained at the old home and tended their flocks and their altar fires.

At least one thing can be said in favor of this theory: In one essential particular it fits the facts. The Oriental mind is essentially submissive and contemplative, while the Occidental mind is essentially aggressive and experimental. Whether in the deep or the shallow places of life, the Oriental lives in a mystical world. In such a world he breathes his native air. Nature to him is a hive of living powers, and is full of surprises. He has always reveled in his mystical contemplation of it, and never faced it as a scholar to whom nothing is too awful; too sacred to be investigated. The love for scientific research has not been altogether strange to his mentality. In their golden days the Arabs did meritorious work as students of science. Nevertheless, the field of exact science does not lie in the East. It is essentially a European sphere which embraces more especially the northern Germanic countries, Italy, France, and England, and, of course, the regions occupied by the descendants of the peoples of those countries in America and other lands. The scientific mind is now invading the East with great force and persistency. Whether it ever will become a permanent characteristic of the easy-going, dreamy Oriental remains to be seen.

Of course, in speaking of the divergent tendencies of the Eastern mind and the Western mind, we must think of the type, and not of the individual. As regards the individual the line of cleavage between the East and the West is not always absolutely definite. There are many restless spirits in the Orient, and many passive and contemplative spirits in the Occident. There are in the former those who have a passion for facts and for exactness in statement, and there are those in the latter who prefer poetry to fact and speculative thinking to the experimental study of nature and of man. The West has produced many mystics and the East many rationalists. Racial and geographical lines seem to form no spirit-tight barriers. Eastern and Western characteristics are often found happily blended in certain individuals who seem to be the earnest of that happier future when the souls of those two worlds shall, let us hope, be joined in spiritual wedlock. For the present, however, and for a long time to come, we are bound to think of the Easterners and the Westerners as two human types differentiated from each other by deep-seated characteristics.

I cannot imagine a group of Orientals forming an expedition for the discovery of the north pole and prosecuting their task with a heroic and dauntless resolution. I cannot think of an Oriental leader undertaking and repeating the adventures of Admiral Peary with a firm determination to win or die. No Oriental, to my mind, could have died the death of Captain Scott in the antarctics. When that heroic Englishman, exhausted and deprived of all means of subsistence, placed his diary under his head against his tent pole and, as a fearless martyr of discovery, awaited the Great Destroyer, he reproduced the whole history of his mighty race.

But I can easily think of an Oriental, or a community of Orientals, looking, praying, and ardently and indefinitely longing for a spiritual vision. I can easily see them traveling the dusty roads of the East with bleeding feet on a pilgrimage to a saint or a shrine. The stories of the shepherds and the Magi in the account of the Nativity reveal the whole soul of the East. A strange star appeared in the heavens and challenged the attention of both the simpleminded shepherds and the learned wise men. It portended a great spiritual event, and, according to the narrative, took its course toward Palestine and the town of Bethlehem.

The heavenly sign was all that was necessary to set the caravan of spiritual seekers in motion. It was all that was necessary to send the shepherds "even to Bethlehem." What are physical discoveries to such minds but of the earth earthy? "Has God visited his people? Let us go then and meet his messenger." They all came to the appointed place to do homage, even to a babe, and to worship.

When Jesus began his ministry he "called disciples" to him by simply saying to certain individuals, "Follow me." They did follow him. They left their occupations, their homes and their parents, and followed Him. The "holy man" held for them a divine mystery. In him and with him there was the possibility of some great spiritual discovery. They followed him, and by so doing set in motion the mightiest spiritual current in history.

In my boyhood days a saint appeared suddenly in a town not far from us near the shore of the Mediterranean. The man had been afflicted for years with what was considered by medical men to be an incurable malady. His limbs were paralyzed so that he could not use them. One morning he was seen to rise and walk like a healthy boy. The news of his recovery without medical assistance thrilled the community and spread far and wide in the Province of Lebanon. The restored man leaped for joy. He declared that, in the night immediately preceding the day of his recovery, Christ came to him, took him by the hand, and bade him arise. Then he felt that all his bonds were loosened and a new supply of life poured into him. The only condition the Great Healer stipulated for him was that he should give all the remaining years of his life to the ministry of religion and to helping the afflicted among his fellow-men.

From various parts of the country people flocked to where the "saint" was, "to receive his blessing." Hundreds of persons afflicted with various diseases were healed by the touch of his hands. A delegation from our own town also went on the holy pilgrimage and returned with glowing reverential reports of the many "mighty works" the saint did in their presence. Thrilling as it was, the event was not considered a new and strange thing under the sun. It was one more evidence of God's nearness to man; another fulfillment of a people's dearest hopes.

Notwithstanding the admixture of fancy and superstition in many of such narratives, they reveal the deepest expectations of the Oriental soul. The phenomena must be studied in their totality. As I shall show later, they must be viewed as the outer shell of the "meat of the word," as the crude setting of the lofty moral and spiritual precepts which the Oriental has given to the world. These are his real discoveries; these are the goal of his adventures and the fruits of his ecstasies, his prayers, and his sufferings.

The Oriental is a quietist, but he is not inert. He is passive, yet heroic. His conquests are in the spiritual realm. His indifference toward the tangible world, which seems cowardly, is born of his enchantment with eternal values. His excessive submissiveness to spiritual visions has deprived him of a better earthly environment and brought upon him many tribulations, yet his comparative estimate of values has merited the respect of mankind. The departure of the Buddha from his royal home into a world of poverty and pain in quest of the Light; the exchange by Moses of the life of a prince for that of a shepherd in order that he might live and die with the people whom he believed God had chosen; the wandering of Jesus in the wilderness for the purpose of achieving final victory over the temptations of life, are incidents which disclose the deepest aspirations of the Eastern soul.

The West also has had its great spiritual conquerors. The story of its missionaries forms a thrilling and ennobling chapter in the annals of the ages. But these missionaries all confess their deep indebtedness to the East. The Eastern scriptures and the cross of Calvary have been to them springs of inspiration and fortitude.

Now the ancient East is being urged by the West to become more aggressive and more scientific than it ever has been or could be. "The modern spirit" is hovering over the East and crying, "Behold, I make all things new." Perhaps it will succeed in effecting such a transformation. But the conditions prevailing in the West are no real encouragement to the East to break away from its ancient moorings. The restlessness of the West calls ever for more restlessness and is straining its nerves to the breaking-point. The West itself is now seeking quiet resting-places, and it finds them not. Amidst the grinding noises of its busy life, mysticism is breaking out in most fantastic shapes. "The ancient wisdom of the East" is being sought, secretly and openly, by millions of Westerners, as a religion of release. It is actually considered a new discovery by many of its seekers and hailed as the way of salvation. This quietist type of mind clashes fiercely with the materialistic tendencies of the times, but it is here as by an irresistible mandate of nature. The frightful wars of this "scientific age" are breeding hosts of "pacifists" and non-resistants. Even in the aggressive West able-bodied men declare that they would rather be killed than fight. Human nature can stand so much pressure, so much excitement and no more. When its way to peace and quiet is blocked in one direction, it seeks another. Saint Augustine's prayer, "O God, Thou hast made us for Thyself, and our heart can find no rest until it find it in Thee," tells the whole story of the human soul.

If the missionaries of the more aggressive life are needed in the East, the missionaries of the more passive life are needed in the West. These two worlds should exchange ideas for the good of both of them. The West is as yet in the process of an experiment. It is trying to ascertain whether man lives to work, or works to live. Whether man cannot tear himself away from the soil and live in a factory; whether he cannot find a "more reasonable" substitute for religion; whether he needs his dreams and visions, or whether he can live solely by the things he can gather into barns.

The experiment has not yet reached its final stage. So far, however, the signs are against, rather than in favor of, an affirmative answer. Despite its external brilliancy, life in the West is increasingly becoming a heavy burden. There is a great deal of intelligent worrying. The fact that the Westerner does not openly bewail his misfortune as much as the Easterner does is no evidence that the misfortunes do not exist. The acid corrodes inwardly, and the evil consequences break out, either in great armed conflicts, or in other forms of "peaceable" fighting between the various interests and classes of society.

From whichever point we may choose to view our subject, we are bound to admit that the dreamy and simple life of the Easterner has not been altogether a mistake. It may be true that "it is better to wear out than to rust out," yet in the end neither state is glorious. There is no inherent reason why the poet and the dreamer should not work with his hands. Even as a poet there is no reason why he should "rust out." He deals with spiritual values whose very nature tends to renew life perpetually. And there is in the end no great glory in dying at the treadmill, without poetry and without dreams; in being driven to death by forces of one's own creation. In fact, to be forced to place before man only these two alternatives of either rusting out or wearing out is a severe condemnation of all human wisdom. If civilized men cannot so live as to avoid either being eaten up by the rust and moth of indolence, or torn up by frenzied activities, then they are worse off than the beasts that perish. Their goal is not life, but death.

Other phases of this subject will be considered in other connections in later chapters. Here it is only necessary to add that the present type of mind, whose dominant word is "Speed," is scarcely a century old. This mere scintilla of time in the long history of man should not be so confidently pitted against all the ages of the past. Good and invigorating as this modern tendency is in some respects, it should not be allowed to veto all the decisions of the former generations. The value of "speed" in all human activity is forever determined by the direction and goal of the march, and not by its heat and perspiration. The Easterner, slow and shabby as he seems to the more active, more aggressive Westerner, has long ago discovered the goal of human life on the earth. The Soul, purified of selfishness and hate, the Soul, with its clear vision of spiritual reality, in perfect control of the world in which it lives, has been to him the Kingdom of God which embraces all values and lies beyond the reach of dissolution and decay.

This man has been slow, even indolent in many ways. His actual achievements remain on the whole far behind his ideal of life. He needs to be quickened to more strenuous effort, and his contact with the West may accelerate his pace as a builder of civilization. But if such contact should tend further to dim his spiritual vision and obscure his goal, the world would certainly be the poorer for it. Progress toward complete emancipation from materialism may be very slow, but it is the only true progress. Here a thousand years may seem but like one day, yet one day of real progress toward such happy consummation outweighs a thousand years of commercial and industrial progress.

Chapter Four – The Symbol of Authority

No less fundamental has been the difference between the Oriental and the Occidental in respect to forms of government. Here what the latter has considered to be fundamental and of permanent worth has been to the former secondary and of transient significance. When one compares the struggles of the Western peoples, especially the Anglo-Saxons, to secure "a free government" and to "establish democracy," with the almost complete indifference of the Easterners to such undertakings, one is led to believe that the Oriental really covets bondage.

With the passive Oriental political revolutions have been very rare. Wherever and whenever they have taken place, they have dealt with temporary crises, and not with the fundamental principles of government. Their results never have been permanent reforms embodied in laws and made to widen the bounds of freedom. The discontent and rebellion of the people in every such case always resulted in an exchange of masters, leaving the laws and the form of government as they were before. The "murmuring" of the people arose against the king, or chief, and some of his satellites, and not against the system which enabled the ruler to oppress his people. The call has always been for a beneficent tyrant, a more merciful king, and not for popular rule. At the present time the Western spirit is finding faint echoes in the East, and the cry for a "civilized government" is being heard in that part of the world, but as yet no tangible results have been secured.

To Westerners, and even to us Westernized Easterners, it would seem that the East is voluntarily sold to bondage. To the Western mind the phrase, "Oriental tyrants," is the embodiment of every accursed thing. It connotes laziness, cruelty, haughtiness, voluptuousness, and every other mean trait and sordid passion. How any people can submit to rulers of this type is to the West a mystery. Think of the Turk enjoying a rule of six hundred years without a single revolution. Think of this "unspeakable" tyrant being called by his people "the shadow of divine providence over the world."

Shortly before I emigrated from Turkey, during the reign of the man whom Gladstone called "Abdul Hamid the Damned," a newspaper in that country had the following to say on the occasion of celebrating the anniversary of its founding:

To-day our paper reaches the thirteenth year of its existence, and we celebrate this anniversary in the reign of the finest pearl of the age and the esteemed center of the universe; at whose grand portal stand the camels of justice and mercy, and to whom the eyes of the kings and the people in the west have been drawn; the rulers there finding an example of political prowess and the classes a model of mercy and kindness; it is our lord and master, the sultan of the two shores and the high king (*Khakan*) of the two seas; the crown of the ages and the pride of all countries, the greatest of all khalifs; the shadow of God on earth; the successor of the apostle of the Lord of the Universe, the victorious conqueror (*Alghazi*), Sultan Abdul Hamid Khan; may God protect his kingdom and place his glory above the sun and moon, and may the Lord supply all the world with the goodness which proceeds from His Holy Majesty's good intentions.

All this is unintelligible to the free peoples of the West. And while Abdul Hamid and the order of things which he represented have for the present passed away to a considerable extent, no new and better order has been established in the land of their former glory.

Unlike this has the Occidental's course been in history. His aggressive tendencies have blossomed in every field of endeavor. His delight has been that of the militant explorer, rather than the subjective thinker; the dauntless assailant of life's obstacles, rather than the passive suppliant before Heaven. And while he has by no means been unmindful of the inner life and the "house not made with hands, eternal in the heavens," he has given his greater energies to the subduing of the earth. In contemplating the wrongs of life, he has not given himself wholly to patience and prayer. His comparatively short history, especially that of the Anglo-Saxon, has been a record of persistent resistance to what he has considered to be evil.

As a nation-builder the Anglo-Saxon has the whole world in his debt. For at least six hundred years he has been the leader of the seekers of political freedom. He has signally triumphed in making the foundations of the State rest on the legitimate, God -given rights of man, woman, and child, and secured the safety of commerce and the freedom of education and of worship.

In attempting to explain the attitude of the Oriental toward this phase of human existence, I do not mean to excuse him. At least I do not mean to say that he has been wholly justified in assuming such a passive attitude toward tyrannical rulers whose line extends from Abdul Hamid to remote antiquity. Political freedom is too precious a thing to me to consider it as of transient value. And although "Democracy" may be worshiped as a term by many, while devoid of content, and superficially idealized by those who would sacrifice nothing to make it real and permanent, I do not consider this sufficient ground to condemn the principle which the term "Democracy" represents.

Yet the Oriental's attitude toward government deserves serious consideration. I feel that he has something of value to say on this subject. The contrast between him and the Occidental is not a contrast between barbarism and civilization, but between two civilizations, the one ancient, the other modern. The Oriental's history comprises millenniums of civilized existence, during which great empires flourished and vanished and great religions were born and highly developed. Architectural wonders bedeck his path through the centuries. The fabrics of his looms have been the pride of kings. His poetry and maxims of wisdom stand majestical in form and supremely rich in thought and feeling. If not the richest, they are certainly among the richest moral and literary treasures of humanity.

The soul which produced all this could not have been that of a savage who had not the capacity for lofty conceptions of human existence, but of a civilized man whose spiritual vision and wisdom successfully searched the deeps of human nature and knew its essential needs. And it is the Oriental's soul that I have in mind, and not certain of his methods. My plea is that this soul should be restored to vigor and productivity along lines congenial to itself and again made to yield rich spiritual harvests.

As a rule the Oriental method of thinking and research has not been the inductive method. The Easterner's deductions and conclusions were not based on wide research and accurate observation of the workings of nature. He has not been a gatherer of what we call "scientific facts." His relation to nature has not been that of an experimental thinker to a body of interrelated objects, but a bond of kinship with the soul of all being. He has been more of a seer and a listener than an aggressive explorer. To discern the purposes of the universe and find in it the paths of spiritual wisdom has been his supreme quest.

With such purpose and methods this "old-fashioned" thinker reached conclusions which are marvelous in their soundness and inclusiveness. He discovered no less than the real value of human life and the things which give the soul ultimate and ennobling satisfaction. However wide the circles of its discoveries and however great the sum of its possessions, the West admits, nor can it reasonably deny, that all these are of relative value. They become of ultimate value and real and serviceable possessions of man only when linked to the Oriental's moral and spiritual discoveries and made subordinate to them. Forms of government, whether monarchical or democratic, are mere methods. They provide a form into which the essence of the life of the community is poured. Of course the form is important but in the last analysis it is the essence, and not the form, which governs. Freedom, suffrage, education, and what not, are conditions under which the individual as he is morally constituted functions. What comes out of the heart is that which ultimately works out man's salvation or damnation.

In his great work, "Modern Democracies" [1] (page 87), Lord Bryce says:

Some have complained that in the Gospel precepts for the conduct of life there is no reference to public or civic duties, unless it be in the saying, "Render unto Caesar the things that are Caesar's." But the answer or explanation seems to be, not only that any such precepts would have been inapplicable (if indeed intelligible) to men living in the political conditions of those to whom the Gospel was first preached, but also that they would have been superfluous. Had Christianity been put in practice, forms of government would have mattered little.

So spoke that great wise man from the West, and in so speaking he gave out the Oriental's secret. If the precepts which the Oriental discovered and formulated centuries ago *were practiced to-day*, forms of government would matter little.

The fact is that the "free" nations of the West are beginning to realize that they have placed too high an estimate on the form and machinery of government. Its great prominence in the minds of men and the costly upkeep of its many and intricate parts threaten to defeat its purpose. It would seem that through politics and legislation in its various forms the peoples are spending more time and effort in self-defense than in self-development. The number of laws increases in geometrical progression. Patriotism is understood by millions in terms of government. The flag is a symbol of government. The peace must be kept by the authority and majesty of the law. War is waged to defend forms of government, and so forth. It would seem also that the end of progress along this line has been reached. It is like traveling around the earth; after one has traveled half the length of the circumference one may keep going, but one's course, then, of necessity leads back to the starting point. Further idealization of the form of government seems to be a waste of time and very costly.

Another distinguished English writer and educator, Dr. L. P. Jacks, Principal of Manchester College, Oxford, and editor of "The Hibbert Journal," said: [2]

The question in which the public interest of all nations is most deeply centred at the present moment is, clearly, that of "government" - a question of Protean forms, but fundamentally the same in them all. It is on the field of politics that the fortunes of mankind are to be ultimately made or lost. Whatever our professions may be, our real belief unquestionably is that to be well "governed" is the supreme need of humanity and that all other needs are secondary to this.

The late war was, in its essence, a dispute as to "who shall be greatest" in the "government" of the world. Shall the world be governed in this way or that, by one set of persons or by another? - such in plain terms was the question at issue. Is there any other question, in the heavens above or on the earth beneath, for the sake of settling which mankind would find it worthwhile to endure such gigantic sacrifices? Is there any other value men prize so highly that to make it good they would pay the price of 12,000,000 slain, 50,000,000 maimed, and a whole continent plunged into economic ruin - to say nothing of the physical, mental, and moral agony of which these things are the symbol? Would it be possible, for example, to get up a war on this scale, or to induce mankind to endure any sort of equivalent sacrifice, for the establishment of the true religion - whatever that may be - or for the moral elevation of the masses, or the extirpation of disease, or for ending the reign of squalor and ugliness? Clearly it would be impossible. Men are willing to endure sacrifices for the things I have named, and very considerable sacrifices, too; but these, taken at their highest, are nothing compared with what they have just endured, and have been enduring for ages, to get the world "governed" according to their liking. What further proof do we need that "government" stands at the top of our scale of values, as the one thing of supreme importance to the world, the thing in which we ultimately *believe* - and this in spite of the fact that after all the unimaginable sacrifices mankind has endured to get itself well governed, the world, as a whole, was never so ill governed, was never in deeper confusion, never drifting so hopelessly to unseen issues? As Dean Inge has recently reminded us, the problem of government, taken in its widest sense, though men have been trying to solve it for five thousand years, still remains unsolved. Nor has the war brought us one hair's-breadth nearer to its solution.

All the same we still retain our belief in "government" as the supreme value, and devote the major part of our resources, material, mental, and spiritual, to the solution of its problems, recurrent wars being the outward and visible signs of our inability to solve them...The effect of the "great" war differed in no essential respect from innumerable lesser wars that preceded it. Instead of solving the problem, it reinstated the problem on another level, and left the struggle for power, the contest as to who shall be greatest, revolving in the vicious circle in which it has never ceased to revolve for five thousand years.

The need for "government," though unquestionably real, is not the primary need of mankind, and all attempts to make it so are doomed to defeat themselves to the end of time. Man's primary need is for *light,* and until this is recognized, and made into a new basis of human relationship, the world will continue to advance from bad to worse on the path of confusion and strife. If these lines should happen to meet the eyes of any man (or woman) who is in search of a life's mission, who is not afraid of immense difficulties, who is willing to devote himself to a cause which is certain to triumph in the end but almost equally certain to involve those who first take it up in defeat, and perhaps in derision - to such a person I would venture to say that he will find the mission he seeks in the effort to break down the political obsession which dominates and poisons the corporate life of the entire Western World.

[1] *Modern Democracies.* (The Macmillan Company, New York.)
[2] *The Literary Review of the New York Evening Post,* February 5, 1922.

Chapter Five - Peace and Freedom

THE wisdom of the East, which is by no means unknown to the West, is highly extolled in the words of the distinguished writer quoted in the previous chapter. "Man's primary need," said Dr. Jacks, "is for *light,* and until this is recognized, and made into a new basis of human relationship, the world will continue to advance from bad to worse on the path of confusion and strife." Again let me say that I do not mean in the least to commend the Oriental's excessive indifference to forms of government. Yet I cannot help wondering whether this spiritual interpreter of human nature and seeker after God could have been of greater service to humanity if he had given himself to the fashioning and refashioning of governmental machinery and the breeding of hosts of politicians, instead of the building of temples and the writing of scriptures. Does not this weary world of ours - weary with the multitude of its external devices - long to-day again to bring its anxious life under the humanizing and soothing sway of those ancient writings? Is it not beginning to realize anew that "man's primary need is for *light*"?

But, it may be asked here, "Have not the political struggles of the Anglo-Saxons been amply justified by their having produced the Magna Charta, the Declaration of Independence, and the American Constitution? Has not democracy given ample justification for its existence and its cost in having produced such a man as Abraham Lincoln?" Yes, these are great and glorious productions. But, on the other hand, has not the Oriental's course in history been justified by the production of the great scriptures? Did not his hopes and aspirations produce such men as Moses and Isaiah? Was is not in the Oriental's home of dreams and visions that the Son of Man and the Twelve walked the earth? - to say nothing of other great Oriental prophets.

Lincoln was great because he succeeded in finding his way to the circle of those ancient seers. He succeeded in emancipating himself from the self-seeking politicians - the by-products of democracy - and giving himself to the law of the Most High. He clasped hands with those revealers of the verities of life as a kindred soul. He succeeded in making the practical wisdom of the Anglo-Saxon serve the ideal wisdom of the entranced seer. Lincoln was not a politician of democracy; he was a prophet of democracy. Like his fellow-prophets of the East, he profoundly realized that "the judgments of the Lord are true and righteous altogether." Like the Great Master, he knew that under whatever form of government malice begets malice and love begets love. When the East and the West meet in the life of humanity as they did in the life of Abraham Lincoln, then the world will have real freedom and lasting peace.

It was for the foregoing reasons - for the fact that he deeply realized that man's primary need is for light - that the Oriental looked upon forms of government as things of secondary importance, as temporary and transient. The supreme importance of the essence made him think very little - perhaps too little of the form. The ruler, or king, has been to him a transient symbol of eternal divine authority. In reality "the Lord is king for ever and ever." "The king's heart is in the hand of the Lord, as the rivers of water; he turneth it whithersoever he will." In a political sense the Oriental has never earnestly cried, "Give me liberty, or give me death." His liberty was to be achieved in the inward man, in the sphere of things which, while not seen, are yet eternal. With him governmental stability was not to be secured by the political vigilance and consent of the governed. "Mercy and truth preserve the king; and his throne is upholden by mercy." Whenever the son of the East has cried against injustice and oppression of rulers, his voice has been directed to the Lord for mercy and to the people for repentance.

Nor has he been a *mere* dreamer. To him God rules the people *through* the people. Neither formal worship nor the vain repetition of prayers, but "righteousness exalteth a nation." "Wash you, make you clean; put away the evil of your doings from before mine eyes; cease to do evil; learn to do well; seek justice, relieve the oppressed judge the fatherless, plead for the widow." Here the eternal Voice speaks to rulers and peoples alike. When both are guided by truth and righteousness, forms of government matter little.

Where do we stand in this "enlightened age"? The great nations of the West are living under democratic forms of government, and the lesser nations are pressing on toward the same goal. We have our municipal, state, and national democracies. We enjoy the freedom of assembly and speech. We have free schools, free churches, and a free ballot. We elect our rulers and bid them carry out our wishes. All such forms and methods are ours as trophies of long political struggles, and we value them most highly. Nay, we would give our lives for their preservation.

And it is because of these things and the other great achievements of the modern mind in the tangible world that the prevailing idea is that we have progressed far beyond the dreams of the people of Isaiah's, and even of Jesus' time. We speak exultingly of our "twentieth-century civilization." We look on the past with a pity tinged with contempt.

But what are the facts? Let us come down to earth and face a stern and disappointing reality. It is no new discovery to say that we are far from living in a beatific state of existence. Such a state remains beyond our imagination. And judging the progress of the future by that of the past it is safe, I think, to say that we are still about two thousand years behind the position which Jesus has marked out for mankind. Dares any one say that our present social order is the state of the pure in heart and the peacemakers? Dares any one assert that we are living to-day in the age of mutual love, mutual forgiveness, and cooperation for spiritual progress? Let a man to-day make such assertions and he would be jeered first of all by the most enthusiastic admirers of our "modern progress."

I am not conscious of the fact that I am a pessimist, nor of any inclination in me to be one. Nor do I wish in the least to convey the impression that our world is morally desolate. Along certain lines humanity has advanced from the position of Jesus' world. We know much more about the laws of nature than the peoples of his time did. We have better schools, better homes, and better clothes than they had. We have achieved, although in a very qualified sense, self-government. Through machinery the forces of nature have become our tools. Our means of communication are miracles of human ingenuity.

But this is not all. We have made further progress, a kind of progress which tends to sober our enthusiasm. Instead of the few laborers in the vineyard of a landlord of Jesus' day, we have a million laborers under an impersonal, mysterious lord called the Company, or the Management. Those ignorant, ancient laborers rejoiced in their tasks; our laborers hate theirs.' All the great barns of the rich man in the Gospel parable could be placed in a corner of one of our warehouses. Our wealth outweighs in the balance the hills of Palestine, and our discontent corresponds with our wealth. In place of the bow and arrow and the limping chariot of the past, we have the armoured train, the airship, the dreadnought, and the eighteen-inch gun. The ancients killed men by the thousands, we kill men by the millions. We can at any time deluge the earth, the sea, and sky with blood and fire.

Verily our progress has been very great, but not symmetrical. On the one side of our nature we are feasting, on the other starved. We are feasting the acquisitive and combative instincts, and starving the religious and altruistic. Our polytechnic schools and commercial establishments are crowded, while our theological schools and churches are only meagerly attended. We have not yet learned, nor do we seem heartily inclined to learn, the eternal fact that "a man's life consisteth not of the things which he possesseth. "We have not learned that a man has nothing if he gains the whole world and loses his own soul. We do not yet realize in our everyday intercourse with one another that if we have all knowledge, but have not love, we are nothing; that a human being is a living soul, and not simply an economic unit; nor do we fully know the meaning of that truly great saying, "Not by might, nor by power, but by my spirit, saith the Lord."

I do not think it is giving way to pessimism to look for a moment on the dark side of things. It is good to face the facts. When we fully analyze the contents of all the new forms we have constructed we shall find that the word "democracy" does not yet connote perfect tranquillity and perfect peace. It is a fine "experiment in government," but has not yet proved a regenerator of human nature. We do elect our officers of state, but after that we are not certain as to what they will do to us. From the turmoil in the commercial and industrial world, we realize that neither our capitalists nor our wage-earners are free and happy men and women. In this "twentieth-century civilization," even in "the land of the free," it is not safe for a woman to go out on the street at night unattended. Our financial institutions are veritable fortresses of concrete and steel and networks of electric "alarms" whose purpose is to protect us, not from the beasts of prey, but from our fellowmen. We cannot agree on a form of religion to be taught in our public schools, and, what is still more sad, we glory in the fact that "the School is divorced from the Church."

In view of all this, and without willfully ignoring the good side of our civilization, one is tempted to say that the wise men from the East were not far wrong in laying the emphasis on human nature itself, rather than on the forms through which it might function. They seem to have known that, when the right spirit ruled men's lives, that spirit would fashion for itself a suitable

29

body to work with. And until that spirit assumed sway, forms of government mattered little. The enthusiastic idealization of forms of government, with all their protecting fleets and armies, involves the grave danger of forgetting the proper contents of those forms.

Of course no reasonable person would from the foregoing draw the inference that there is no difference between a dynastic monarchical form of government and a republic, or a democracy. That to be ruled by men claiming to exercise authority by divine right is the same as to be ruled by laws freely enacted by a people's chosen representatives and administered by officers directly responsible to the people. No. There are inherent reasons which make a representative form of government more conducive to progress than a dynastic system. Such reasons are so obvious as to need no mention in such work as this. And the call of the hour is not for a return to monarchical or feudal systems of government, but for an advance toward real democracy.

The skilled and efficient builder of the machinery of government is, of course, an obvious necessity. The enactment of laws to meet the needs of a progressive social order is another. However, no nation can afford to be so engrossed in the construction of governmental machinery and so enmeshed in its multitude of legal enactments as to kill out its dreamers of dreams and seers of visions. No nation's universe should be rendered so mechanical as to make God Himself a stern judge, or a law-bound chief of police, instead of a Spirit of truth and love. Government never can be an external system. It is a mode of life. And life never can find full expression or full satisfaction in its mechanical devices. Man is a spirit as God is a spirit. Ultimately man's freedom, peace, and security must be achieved within.

The present state of this modern world demands most urgently a union of souls between the wise men of the East and the wise men of the West. The dreamer and the practical thinker must be joined into one and thus of the twain make one new man - a man that is fit to rule himself and to possess the earth. What a splendid programme the ancient Oriental seer has for the present civilization. What a fine "Americanization" programme for both the native-born and the foreign-born. "Wash you, make you clean; put away the evil of your doings from before mine eyes; cease to do evil; learn to do well; seek justice, relieve the oppressed, judge the fatherless, plead for the widow." There is a prophetic call to living men, to the units of which nations are made. The supreme need is for the intensive cultivation of the spirit of true democracy, the spirit of fraternity and cooperation for progress in all that makes life true, good, and beautiful.

Chapter Six - Leaders

At such times as the present it is very natural that the cry for "leaders" should be heard everywhere. The "great men of the past" are called to remembrance and their like deeply longed for. This is very natural, because leadership, or rule by delegated or assumed authority, is an inherent necessity in the life of any group. It is found to be so among flocks of birds, herds of cattle, savage tribes, feudal states, monarchies, as well as in the most advanced republics. The focusing of the life of the group in a leader is not a matter of theory; it is so seemingly by the compulsion of nature. The effectiveness and safety of the group depend in the largest measure upon good leadership.

Again the acknowledgment of and the submission to a leader is an expression of hero-worship which is one of man's noblest traits. Hero-worship is a cry of desire. Its sense is prophetic. Through it the common man exercises himself into greatness. Largely because of it the common man believes that "the best is yet to be." In the great leader he sees the first fruits of a nobler race. He beholds his own personality breaking through its limitations and going from strength to strength as if its capacity for growth were infinite. To him the great leader is an assurance and guarantee that despite all its weaknesses humanity cannot be pronounced a failure. Judged by its best fruits this defective human nature can still be called divine. The presence of the great leader is a powerful, heartening incentive for the common man to press on toward the prize of a noble self-fulfillment. It is a spring of inspiration for every mother to hope that to her a child may be given who shall be called great.

It is no wonder that throughout the ages great men have been revered as the incarnation of deity. They have seemed to gather in themselves the hopes and the aspirations of all the years and to triumph over all the ills which befall man upon the earth.

So the leader has always been expected to be strong, diligent, true, and just, as truth and justice have been known and appreciated by the successive generations. Whether under kings or presidents, the people have never directly ruled themselves and it seems certain that they never can. The leader has always been expected to guide his people into a beatific state of existence and to bear all their sins.

And it is not altogether paradoxical that as the leaders of peoples have enjoyed all the glory, they have also experienced all the humiliation of which the human mind has had knowledge. They have enjoyed the applause of assemblies and the acclaims of nations and have suffered the most corroding criticisms and been driven by the hooting crowds into inglorious obscurity. All this is very familiar to all peoples. Nor is it due to "the ingratitude of republics"; it is much older than they. It is so old that its significance is expressed in the maximal sayings of the ancient East. One of those sayings is, "The head [symbolizing the leader] has many aches."

The turning of peoples against their leaders is not only natural, but is born also of idealism, and not of sordid passion. It expresses the disappointment of hope, real or imaginary. "To whom much is given, from him much [often too much] is required. "A leader's failure seems to be the failure of a people's light, nay, the collapse of a people's own noblest powers. All the prophecies which they had perceived fulfilled in him have proved false, and the spirit which had spoken to them through him proved a lying spirit.

It is a very normal thing to cry for leaders and deliverers. It is also a normal thing, although it may be at times a cruel thing, to criticize the leaders and bring them to judgment as the stewards of the people.

But what the people as a whole seldom if ever realizes is the fact that a leader is born of his people's soul, and that what a people sows that also it shall reap. A prophet is the offspring of generations of prayer and spiritual aspirations, and as such he never fails. The eternal years are his. But let me at present limit myself to political and social leadership which is the demand of the times. In the present confusion, the cry is for "real statesmen" to pull this world out of the mire of despair. The people as' a whole seldom if ever realizes that a leader, or a statesman, represents the average wisdom and the average virtue of the people as a whole. This is true especially in a democracy in which the leader is chosen by the multitude to act, not as a prophetic pathfinder, but as the representative of the "wishes of his constituents." It is often forgotten that the leader of a flock of geese is a goose, and the leader of a herd of buffaloes is a buffalo. He may be a strong individual, nevertheless he is one of the flock or herd in whom the essential qualities of his followers are represented.

Even if the representative of any particular constituency is a very superior individual, if he is to be a leader he cannot march much faster than the average speed of his group. He may be able to speak idealistic words and to utter noble prophecies, yet, when he attempts to convert his words into deeds, he comes against the average mind of the times and can do no more than that mind will allow. So I think, if we make an accurate survey of our governmental agencies from the Board of Aldermen in our towns and cities, with all their satellites of ward politicians and shopkeepers, through our State Legislatures and up to the National Congress, we shall find that the average wisdom and virtue of those leaders is no higher than that of the collective wisdom and virtue of the people who elected them. [1]

Leaders are born of the soul of their people. Consciously and unconsciously they reflect the glory and the shame of the social group. When the people criticize their statesmen, they are simply looking at their own face in a mirror. The unfriendly rivalries of the business interests, the suspicions which put the individuals in everyday life on the defensive toward one another, church quarrels, the indifference to spiritual idealism in the home and the office, and individual selfishness of every sort, all enter into the very texture of government. They creep across the national borders and create international disputes. They and they only call for huge armaments for "defensive purposes." Under such conditions, as of old, any half a dozen statesmen of different nations, quarrelling among themselves and supported by as many great editors, can lead their nations into war in a very short time.

What is the type of leader that is being sought to-day? This seeking also is not a matter of theory and design. It is always a people's desire mysteriously born, which finally determines the character of their choice. The activities of life always precede any philosophy of life, and the necessities and problems of a people come in advance of the theories and means necessary for their solution. The modern world's great problems are economic and are born of the vast expansion of its material life. Technical and professional skill is deemed the pressing need of the hour. The cry is for great leaders in the worlds of politics, science, invention, finance, industry, commerce. The coils of the economic interests of life are increasingly tightening with the passing of time and the increase of wealth, so that the cry everywhere is for saviors from what seems to be the imminent economic strangulation of society. This fear may be exaggerated, but it certainly prevails.

Of this necessity leaders, or would-be leaders are being born. We have great financiers, great captains of industry; great politicians, great business men, and great scientists.

There is no lack of remedial formulas, no lack of effort to bind the world's wounds, to clothe it and restore it to its right mind. The economists are hard at work devising short cuts to the stabilization of credit and the revival of industry. The statesmen are flitting hither and thither pouring the oil of their wisdom upon the troubled waters and drawing new maps and charts for the future course of civilization. The chemists, biologists, sociologists, and mathematicians are also putting their talents at the disposal of this afflicted world. It would seem that the wisdom of this world should be sufficient to give it prosperity and tranquillity.

Our statesmen are making treaties and forming gentlemen's agreements as bonds of international good will; our economists find the remedy of our ills in more production and better distribution of commodities; our biologists recommend selective breeding and the elimination of the unfit; and our mathematicians insist on the "technologizing" of all our activities.

The last-mentioned and very alluring remedy has been recently offered with a great flourish by Alfred Corzybski in a book entitled "Manhood of Humanity." [2] The author claims to have discovered a new law of "human engineering" which opens a new era in the life of mankind. The application of this law is deemed sufficient to cure all our ills.

Count Corzybski's "new discovery" is of two parts. First, that man is neither an animal nor a supernatural being. He is a natural being. Of course this is not new. The evolutionists have been preaching this doctrine for three quarters of a century. The advanced spiritual thinkers of to-day find in man a representation of the soul and body of the universe. To them "natural" and "supernatural" are no different from "seen" and "unseen" or "tangible" and "intangible." Nor do we differentiate man from the animal by simply calling him natural. The animal is a natural being, indeed.

Second, the Count has discovered that man is a time-binder. The plant is a matter or a chemical-binder; the animal is a space-binder; man is a time-binder. The plant can gather matter into itself, but cannot roam in space. The animal can roam in space, but has no conception of time. Man has the faculty for living in both space and time; that is, he accumulates experience and profits by it. He can bring the past forward, make it serve the present, and extend the benefits of both the past and the present into the future.

It appears, however, that this "discovery" was known even to the serpent which gave advice to our first parents. In the story of the creation we find that the serpent "said unto the woman, yea, hath God said, Ye shall not eat of every tree of the garden? And the woman said unto the serpent, We may eat of the fruit of the trees of the garden; but of the fruit of the tree which is in the midst of the garden, God hath said, Ye shall not eat of it, neither shall ye touch it, lest ye die. And the serpent said unto the woman, Ye shall not surely die; for God doth know that in the day ye eat thereof, then your eyes shall be opened, and ye shall be as gods, knowing good and evil." Here we have a most striking illustration of "time-binding" on a large scale. That man can look backward and forward has been a commonplace fact to all generations. Therefore the phrase, "time-binding," contains no revolutionary idea.

What does Count Corzybski make of his "new discovery"? He puts the essentials of his programme for the securing of happiness for all mankind in a short paragraph which he repeats in his book in one form or another very frequently. "Humanity," he says on page 74, "in order to live, must produce creatively and therefore must be guided by applied science, by technology; and this means that the so-called social sciences of ethics, jurisprudence, psychology, economics, sociology, politics, and government must be emancipated from medieval metaphysics; they must be technologized; they must be made to progress and to function in the proper dimension - the human dimension and not that of animal; they must be time-binding sciences."

This is precisely what the Western world has been doing with great persistency for at least two hundred years. Technologizing has been its driving passion. And it was this sort of time-binding activity which gave us the Germany of the Kaiser and his foresighted, or time-binding advisers. Count Corzybski does bring in Germany as a shining example of technological efficiency, although he does not excuse her onslaught against civilization. However, he fails, I think, to appreciate the force of the motive behind the technologizing skill.

To him, if only the generations of men would keep up the "geometric progression" uninterrupted by wasteful activities, we should have a happy world. If each generation would take up progress at the point where the preceding generation left off, conserving the fruits of the past and bequeathing that and the increase caused by its own efforts to the future, all would be well. Scientific production progressing geometrically and a perfect system of distribution would give the world its longed-for millennium.

All this is good and serviceable so far as it goes. The services which science is rendering and may yet render to man by extending his dominion over nature and freeing his body from disease and his mind from error cannot be

34

overestimated. But man's *personality,* with all its motives and passions out of which his gravest problems arise, lies deeper than any scientific engineering can reach. It does not seem possible that the "manhood of humanity" can be attained by the mere exercising of its skill. Thus far human experience does not bear out such an assertion. Thus far we find that the greater the means of production and distribution and the more scientific the methods of human thinking, the more vexing are humanity's social problems. It is no mere guessing that we can be very accurate thinkers and still hate one another: that we can have the highest diplomatic skill and yet use it to deceive one another, and the highest scientific skill and yet use it to kill one another.

With the progress of time-binding technologization wars are becoming more and more devastating; the tenement, the apartment, and the restaurant are taking the place of the home; the cohesion of the family is loosening; class contentions are becoming more severe, and the temples of worship are well-nigh deserted. Evidently there is something more fundamental that is needed than the making of treaties, the elimination of the unfit, and the technologizing of human efforts. The need is for a concept of life which shall embrace those moral values, so elusive to experimental science, and direct them so as to guide man in all his intellectual endeavors: a concept which no man can hold and remain a misanthrope.

What is really needed as a basic principle for the prosperity and the tranquillizing of human society is the spiritual vision, the courage for humanity to face its nobler ideals and put them into practice. Whether man is a natural or a supernatural being may be a matter of pure knowledge. The *dynamic* fact is the recognition of the soul - whatever it may be to the speculative thinker - as superior to all its possessions. The kind of "human engineering" that is needed is not only that which gives man wider control of natural forces and resources, but that which makes a man think of his fellow-men as a community of spiritual beings too sacred to be invaded either by the ruthless builders of great fortunes or by cannon and the sword. The time-binding faculty in man may be a blessing or a curse according as he evaluates his fellow-men; according as to whether they are to him economic possibilities to be exploited, or spiritual possibilities to be brought into full realization. Jesus and Napoleon were among the greatest time-binders in history. Yet how vastly different have their purposes and achievements been in their bearing on human well-being.

The dreamy East has spoken it, "Where there is no vision the people perish." The man of vision, who is not only a far-sighted time-binder, regardless of motive, but a prophet whose kingdom is not of this world, must be the people's leader. Of course the enraptured prophet is not a very suitable individual to head a financial institution or to watch the pulse of the stock exchange. As a rule this type of man needs others to provide him with the necessities of life. But it is his vision which gives lasting value to all human possessions, intellectual and material. The talents of other leaders in the world of industry > commerce, finance, education, and politics are great and beneficent forces. Their possessors deserve humanity's profound gratitude and esteem. But the values of their achievements remain relative, partial, transient, until they are related to the prophet's vision; then they put on immortality. Then the labors of the hands and the brain become prayers, and the concept of life a holy ideal lifting it above the petty and mean concerns of selfishness and sordid passion. Only such a vision of our life individual and social, national and international, can guard the purity of the youth, the chastity of men and women, promote honesty of thought, purity of motive, make of the family abode a home of love, instead of a cooperative boarding-house, and promote just, honest, and peaceable dealing between men and nations. Our first and greatest leader is he who is able to teach us the language of a spiritual universe in which God and the Soul are the source and guarantee of all values.

The East has given the world, not its only leaders, but its chief leaders in this field of vision. "Up from undated time they come," and out of the soul of that mystical Asia which now looks to the West, not for the iron rod of the conqueror, but for the helping hand of the grateful friend.

[1] To anticipate any objection by the reader to this statement, which was once challenged when I made it in a public address, I will quote the following: "The want of respect for legislatures is due to the quality of the men who fill them, few of whom are superior in knowledge and intelligence to the average of their fellow citizens, and many of whom are (in some States) below that average in point of character." (Lord Bryce in *Modern Democracies*, quoted above, vol. II, p. 155.)
[2] *Manhood of Humanity.* (E. P. Dutton & Company, New York.)

Part Two - Religious and Social Tendencies in the East and in the West

Chapter Seven - What of Religion?

IF it ever was difficult to define religion, it certainly is so to-day. It seems to "be impossible, in these days of intellectual ferment and revolution, to give a generally acceptable definition of religion. Thought shifts basis so quickly that any definition in the religious and ethical world becomes old while in process of construction.

It may be no reflection on the present to call it the agree-to-differ age. This description implies at least tolerance. Ours is the age of variety. The theist and the humanist, the deist and the pantheist, the supernaturalist and the naturalist, the materialist and the spiritualist, the vitalist and the pragmatist, are all with us. They are all out in print. They have also the privilege of the platform and the pulpit, free and unrestricted. The granting of this freedom and equal opportunity to decent thought, expressed in a decent and orderly manner, is one of the most desirable features of modern times.

A critical presentation of any and all of those -*isms* falls outside the purpose of the present work. So far as can be seen, they all circle around the central thought of religion at various distances. Each one of them claims to be the truth and nothing but the truth, although not each one claims to be the whole truth, as yet. But they give no definition of religion which is acceptable alike to all of their respective adherents. The failure should not, I think, be considered a calamity. However important a definition of religion may be to speculative theology, to the vast majority of worshipers it practically does not exist. No human soul ever seeks to put itself in tune with the Infinite on the basis of a definition of religion. Religious experience antedates all definitions of religion, as thinking antedates all psychology, and the vital processes precede all physiology. The word "religion" remains well understood by all intelligent persons until some one undertakes to define it. Then the confusion of tongues begins. To know all the current definitions of religion is not to know very much. Such information is more likely to bewilder than to reassure its possessor.

The story of the sexton of a chapel in a great university throws much light on this point. From youth to old age this humble commoner listened to the preaching of distinguished scholars from all over the world. It seems that there was no lack of definition of religion in the great sermons. One day a visitor at the university while chatting with the sexton after the morning service said to him, "You have been hearing great scholarly preaching here for many years." "Yes, sir," said the sexton: "I have listened to preaching in this chapel for forty years, and, thank God, I am still a Christian."

The great influence of the Bible over the minds of men in all walks of life is due in no small measure to the fact that it is not a book of definitions. It is the evidence of the workings of religion, rather than a statement of its technique. And no amount of definition the human mind can construct will ever be able to give so clear an idea of religion as the Great Book presents. Throughout his long history the Oriental has been first of all a seer. In the great scriptures he reports his visions of the eternal realities with childlike simplicity. He may not be correct in all his descriptions of those realities, but he certainly has apprehended and felt "the Soul that maketh all." The enlarging vision of God, the strength of faith, the dignity of worship, the victory of prayer, the power of righteousness, the sovereignty of truth, and the sweetness of love, have all seemed to him too obvious to be missed, and too great to be defined. His simple declarations, "In the beginning was God," "God is our refuge and strength," "Righteousness exalteth a nation," "Create in me a clean heart, O God, and renew a right spirit within me," "What doth the Lord require of thee, but to do justly, and to love mercy, and to walk humbly," "Blessed are the pure in heart, for they shall see God," "Seek ye first the kingdom of God and his righteousness," "Now abideth faith, hope, love, these three, and the greatest of these is love" - these, to quote no others, are the transcendent meditations of the human soul. Like the stirrings of love in the heart, they do not need to be defined in order to be known and appreciated. Any definition of religion which does not connect with these elemental thoughts is a hollow sound.

Long ago, the Oriental discovered and the Occidental recognized, in all the varieties of his religious opinions, that religion speaks the language of completeness. All other human activities deal with partial things and with relative values. The religious act is all-embracing. It is the act of the soul in its totality. It is the drawing of the finite with all his concerns, all his joys and all his sorrows, toward the Infinite. Anything short of this may not be necessarily bad, but is incomplete. It may be seeking of knowledge, directing the course of politics, conducting a legitimate business, administering relief to the sick and the needy, or any other approved interest. Yet none of these things can by any ingenious method be elevated to the dignity of religion. All such interests have value only in relation to man. Man finds his ultimate value, not in the world of technical education nor of politics, nor of business, nor even of philanthropy, but in his conscious relation to the World-Life, the Universal Soul - God!

If the other activities of life than those which are strictly religious tend to make the way to this ultimate goal more clear; if they serve to give the spiritual power of man a wider application in the affairs of life; if they further a deeper appreciation by a man of the spiritual value of his fellowmen, then they can be properly entered as assets in the book of life. Otherwise they may be liabilities. As partial interests they may usurp the place of completeness, and as relative values they may impede the progress of their possessor toward the ultimate goal of his being.

Thus the great books of religion give us a practical definition of it in terms of life. So our Bible teaches. The noblest passages of this book awaken us to the presence of a divine Reality. Religion is our endeavor to find ourselves with all our interests of whatever description within the divine realm. Our driving and guiding forces toward this goal are love, service, worship. The name of your ism may be whatever you wish it to be. I find, however, from your attitude toward the mystery of being and from your literature that your supreme purpose is to shake yourself down into an equilibrium in the embrace of this universe. Call it Nature, Life, Motion, Ether, Electricity, God. If you are alive at all and thinking beneficently, you are seeking the Eternal, and your soul can find no rest until it find it in Him.

With regard to this inescapable fact, I find no difference between the East and the West. The infinite mystery overshadows both of them. But the difference (as will appear in the following chapters), which is no small one, is to be found in the method of approach to this mystery. This I call no small difference, because the road chosen may be such as to cause the seeker to lose himself in the wilderness.

Chapter Eight - Man Is Not Incurably Religious

THERE is a current saying which was apparently established as a truth by a hasty generalizer, despite the facts. It is the saying that "man is incurably religious." When such a generality roots itself in the public mind, it becomes fairly well sheltered from critical examination. It becomes the slogan of the over-enthusiastic preacher on the one hand and the indolent religionist on the other.

There seems to be no insurmountable difficulty involved in an opposite estimate of man's religious nature. He may be said to be incurably irreligious and a chronic backslider.

It is difficult to see how any careful observer can, in the face of present-day religious statistics, assert that man is incurably religious. The universal complaint of religious teachers in America, as well as other countries, to-day is that the majority of the people are unchurched and have no active interest in religion.

Nor is this state of things wholly new. From the past comes the cry of Isaiah against Israel: "Hear, O heavens, and give ear, O earth, for the Lord hath spoken; I have nourished and brought up children, and they have rebelled against me. The ox knoweth his owner, and the ass his master's crib; but Israel doth not know, my people doth not consider. Ah, sinful nation, a people laden with iniquity, a seed of evildoers, children that deal corruptly; they have forsaken the Lord, they have despised the Holy One of Israel, they are estranged and gone backward." When we add to this John the Baptist's designation of the people of his day as a "generation of vipers," Jesus' calling of those same people "an evil and adulterous generation," and the cry of such heralds of faith as Savonarola, Luther, Wesley, and others against the irreligiousness of their times, we can in no way be justified in speaking of man as being incurably religious.

Not long ago, addressing a meeting of religious workers in New York, Dr. John H. Finley, Commissioner of Education of the State of New York, had this to say about the religious condition of that city:

The tide of materialism and paganism seems about to overwhelm the first city of the Republic. Even the Roman Church, as the most recent figures reveal, has lost nearly two hundred thousand adherents in the last ten years. It does not mean that they are becoming Protestants; it means that they are becoming pagans. There are more than two million Jews in Greater New York, and yet all the synagogues put together have a seating capacity, when filled, of hardly more than two hundred thousand. Thus the leaders of the Jewish Church reach only a fraction of their own people. The Protestant membership of all New York churches is about ten per cent of the population, with about a million people of Protestant antecedents unattached and apparently unreachable. [1]

Such a state of things is by no means peculiar even to New York City.

It is also very evident that man's religious progress has not kept pace with his intellectual and political progress. Man as a worshiper of God and contemplator of spiritual realities has yielded large territories to man as the builder of an earthly kingdom. And not the least of the evidences of the dimness of modern man's spiritual vision is his growing belief that large and sanitary cities, vast and well-regulated industries, and the great daring of scientists, explorers, and engineers are worthy substitutes for religion.

Of course, if we were to speak so indifferently we might say that man is incurably musical, incurably literary, incurably poetical, simply because there are always musicians, literary men and poets of one kind or another in human society. But the fact is that man is not anything incurably. He comes nearer to being incurably acquisitive than anything else.

In view of all this, it seems to me that it is more correct to say that the religious sense is a native element in human nature, which must struggle for its life, than to say that man is incurably religious. In other words, the mere existence of the religious sense in *man* is no sure guarantee of its growth and dominance over the other great interests in the lives of *individual men*. It can be assigned a minor place on life's programme, or even forgotten altogether and swallowed up by other and inferior interests.

By saying this, I am not aware of the slightest intention on my part to belittle man's religious potentialities or their importance in the shaping of his destiny. On the contrary, I assert that man never can be complete until he is completely religious. But I do assert that the religious sense in man has not been arbitrarily favored by the creative Spirit, but, like any other faculty, has been destined to struggle for supremacy. This I consider to be testimony to the vitality and greatness of religion. And it should be a source of gratification to every preacher and teacher of religion to realize that his fight for godliness in the world is a real and not a sham fight: to know that the desired victory in the struggle of truth with error and righteousness with sin has not been foreordained, but must be won by hard and heroic fighting. The unorganized religious sense is a heritage of the type; but religion as an active force in the affairs of life is an individual achievement. Our unearned inheritance from the World-Life is the shapeless plastic material, but not the finished product. The universe has no spiritual almshouse in it. Within its confines every great attainment has its corresponding cost. Nor is the freedom of choice ever denied to man. The wide gate and the broad way which lead to destruction, and the strait gate and the narrow way which lead to life, are forever open to him.

The ancients knew all this. The voice of the Oriental scriptural writer rings as clear and true to-day as it did thousands of years ago: "I call heaven and earth to witness against you this day, that I have set before thee life and death, the blessing and the curse; therefore choose life, that thou mayest live, thou and thy seed."

The Oriental's spiritual seeking has by no means been constant and unremitting. This failure may be said to be human in its extent. But it may be truly said that, with all his failures, stumblings, and fallings, the Oriental has been a *spiritual* seeker. "The law of the Lord," as the Easterner has been able to understand it, has been his "meditation day and night." Religion to him is the highest form of truth. To know this truth is to be admitted into the secret of all being. This ancient attitude toward spiritual reality has been finely stated by a noted British scholar. [2]

Man's religion [said Professor Caird] is the expression of his ultimate attitude to the universe, the summed-up meaning and purport of his whole consciousness of things. . . . Whatever else religion may be, it undoubtedly is the sphere in which man's spiritual experience reaches its utmost concentration, in which, if at all, he takes up a definite attitude toward his whole natural and spiritual environment. In short, it is the highest form of his consciousness of himself in his relation to all other things and beings; and, if we want a brief abstract and epitome of the man, we must seek for it here or nowhere.

It is said that, while the Oriental has been absorbed in religion as the highest form of truth, he has not sufficiently moralized it. That his duty as a social being has not been so scrupulously performed as has been his duty as a religious being, and that his moral life rests on a much lower level than his religious life. There is much truth in this statement, although the failure described above may be said to be humanity's at large, and not only the Oriental's. The perfect blending of pure religion and a lofty morality has not yet been attained by any people. It is obvious also that it is much easier to go through the form of a prayer than to do justly, to love mercy, and to walk humbly. The Oriental has not been unmindful of all this. His precept, "Thou shalt love the Lord thy God with all thy heart, and thy neighbor as thyself," marks the highest elevation of both religion and morality. He has always known that worship offered as a bribe to God to connive at the worshiper's moral delinquency was "an abomination." The individual is to be not only morally respectable, but to be holy as God is holy.

Nevertheless, it is true that the Oriental has unduly emphasized the transitoriness of this life, with all its political and social institutions, and sympathized too greatly with the frailties of human nature. It is true also. that the Anglo-Saxon has rationalized and moralized religion to a far greater degree than the Easterner has. But the difference here does not arise from the fact that the Easterner thinks less highly of morality than the Anglo-Saxon does. The Easterner's literature and his reverential regard for "righteous men" preclude such an inference. The real cause is the fact that a thorough consideration of details in almost any field of thought has never been an Oriental characteristic. Whether in agriculture, industry, commerce, education, or any other sphere, the son of the East considers sustained systematic endeavor a sort of bondage. Life for him is a natural thing. It should be allowed to function naturally and joyously. Undue interference with its processes tends to defeat its purpose. What is *nearly* complete is satisfactory to him.

The Anglo-Saxon almost worships system and order. The thorough application of a principle is an overmastering passion with him. To the typical Oriental the Anglo-Saxon mind is a "one-track mind."

But there is still another difference here. To the Oriental moral defects and intellectual inaccuracies must never be allowed to estrange a man from religion. With him it is need, and not merit, which leads the soul to the altar. The distinction between a "good moral man" and a "religious man" is unknown to him. The individual is complete when he is one with God. To this fountain of grace he must come with all his moral infirmities. A code of morals is good as a by-product of this surrender of the soul to its Maker, but as a man-made thing it rests on a vacuum.

It has, indeed, been a most fortunate thing for the world that the Oriental never allowed himself to give up the writing of scriptures and the building of temples because of his moral weaknesses and intellectual inaccuracies.

On the other hand, the progress of the Occidental, especially the Anglo-Saxon, is characterized by an increasing tendency to make intellectual accuracy and moral rectitude prerequisites of religious fellowship. An irregularity in his moral conduct is very likely to lead him to leave the Church. This is the defect of a great virtue. The moral aim here is so lofty that it tends to defeat its own purpose. The respectable Anglo-Saxon feels that he must not claim to be what he really is not. Furthermore, the complex relations of his life at times necessitate transactions which to him do not seem altogether ideal. So it would seem that this individualistic, calculating Westerner wants to be able to say in certain circumstances, "I do not profess to be a religious man," even though he may be conscious of the fact that such a statement *explains,* rather than *excuses,* his position. And if it is true that according to present-day standards the religion of the Oriental is not sufficiently moral, it is equally true that the Occidental's morality is becoming more and more Godless.

It would be well for us to realize first as last that however cunning he may be man cannot outwit the universe. There is a higher law which forever nullifies all laws which clash with it. Man can no more have a sound, potent, and stable morality without God than he can have a science without the physical world. Just as a scientific fact is the correct apprehension by the mind of an act of nature's, so a moral fact is the correct realization by the whole man of the functioning of the moral law. Man does not make his moral possibilities; he discovers them; and, if he will, conducts himself in such a way as to bring them into full realization. The source of his moral life is both within him and above him, and that source is God.

If the world is to have a moral religion and a religious morality, the wise men from the East and the wise men from the West must together form one communion. And if in this communion religion is given the place of honor, then it will be a communion of saints. Then morality will have an abiding foundation, and religion a wider human environment in which to function. Then the highest form of truth by which men actually live spiritual truth will be the central sun around which all the interests of life will revolve.

All nations know [says Hegel] that it is the religious consciousness in which they possess the truth; and they have therefore regarded their religion as that which gives dignity and peace to their lives. All that awakes doubt and perplexity, all sorrow and care, all limited interests of finitude, we leave behind us on the "bank and shoal of time." And, as on the summit of a mountain, removed from all hard distinctness of detail, we calmly overlook the limitations of the landscape and the world, so by religion we are lifted above all the obstructions of finitude. In religion, therefore, man beholds his own existence in a transfigured reflexion, in which all the divisions, all the crude lights and shadows of the world, are softened into eternal peace under the beams of a spiritual sun. It is in this native land of the spirit that the waters of oblivion flow, from which it is given to Psyche to drink and forget all her sorrows; for here the darkness of life becomes a transparent dream-image, through which the light of eternity shines in upon us. [3]

[1] Quoted from *The Christian Century.*
[2] Edward Caird, in *The Evolution of Religion,* vol. I, p. 30. (James Maclehose and Son, Glasgow.)
[3] Quoted by Edward Caird in *The Evolution of Religion,* vol. I, p. 82. (James Maclehose and Son, Glasgow.)

Chapter Nine - Holy Books

WHILE in Paris during the Peace Conference, when the atmosphere of that historic city was thick with pessimism, a noted American newspaper correspondent sought to convince me that Western civilization was on its way to the grave.

"You may be proud and grateful," he said to me, "that you are an Easterner. Your people have given the world nine things which will live as great truths as long as humanity endures. The West has given itself to the building-up of a material civilization which is now being shattered by its own forces. Theorize as we may, Western civilization is practically dead."

"You do not mean all you say," I answered. "Certainly at present Europe is in a sad condition, but what of America? You do not mean that American civilization is practically dead?"

"No," said he, "but it is on the way. The same symptoms of decay which are so pronounced in the case of Europe are being increasingly manifested in American life. Western civilization is doomed."

I did not quite agree with my friend, not even with regard to Europe. I had to admit that the better tendencies of Western civilization were hard-pressed by contrary forces, but could not agree that the ultimate defeat of this civilization was so evident and so near. While I felt, and feel, proud of the fact that the East has given the world its "holy books" which deal with those spiritual realities without which no true civilization can be achieved, I did not, and do not, think that in this respect the West has been altogether barren. Of course no people is too great to perish when its spiritual vision fails. The West to-day sorely needs to dwell on this fact. It is too absorbingly engaged in trafficking in material things and is weakening its spiritual security by overemphasizing the importance of its technical skill.

Nevertheless, the spiritual treasures of humanity have been committed to the exclusive keeping of no one race or people. Nor is religious truth to be found only within these books of the various peoples which are known as "holy scriptures." The spirit of prophecy is in reality a human and not a racial heritage, and canonized holy books are not the only spiritual achievements credited to mankind.

The races which produced those great scrolls of destiny may be said to have attained the summits of spiritual thinking, yet those who could scale only the lower heights cannot be denied the claim to being fellow-heirs with those deep-visioned seers of the ages.

In a large sense the East and West are spiritual kinfolk and joint heirs. Yet, whatever the East may have to borrow from the West, one thing is certain. The students of religion in the Western world must forever turn their eyes toward the East. It is the mystical background of spiritual contemplation and the chief medium of transmission of what the world knows as divine truth.

That all the great living scriptures, from the Rigveda to the Koran, originated in Asia could not have been a mere accident. Nor can we ascribe to an accidental occurrence at some point in history the passionate desire and ceaseless endeavor of the Western world to convert nature's forces into commercial values. Deliberate choice must have had a large share in causing the wide divergence between the Western mind and the Eastern mind, and deliberate choice only can bring them into harmony. Neither accident nor an arbitrary act of a higher power can fuse the gifts of the various races together nor force the individual to conserve and cherish the better heritage of the race. Only he who seeks shall find.

The Oriental's achievements in history could not have been the products of mere instinct. He fully knew and appreciated the significance of the course he chose in life. He seems to have weighed in the balance the advantage of dealing with nature's body and that of dealing with nature's soul, and to have chosen the latter. As his great maxims of wisdom show, he knew the power of wealth, the glory of authority, and the pride of knowledge, and deliberately gave all these things a subordinate place in the plan of life. The fact that the East has for these many centuries maintained religion as the center of its life has not been due to the fact that every Oriental is a saint and a prophet, nor to the supposition that man is incurably religious, but to the fact that the conception of life by both the great and the small has been first and last religious. Perfect or imperfect, rich or poor, wise or simple, the Oriental *as a type* has always clung to the horns of the altar. To him the divine spirit forever hovers compassionately over the heights and depths of life. His deepest being stands revealed to the eye of Heaven. With deep and reverential awe he cries to the Eternal, "Whither shall I go from thy Spirit? or whither shall I flee from thy presence?" Neither the heights nor the depths nor the darkness could hide him from the One who never slumbers nor sleeps.

Notwithstanding his great antiquity, the Oriental has never allowed scientific investigation to dissipate his mystical sense. The First Cause has been his enchanter. Immediate or secondary causes seem never to have been of compelling interest to him. All so-called natural occurrences around and within him have been to him direct acts of God. Rain and wind, thunder and lightning, growth and decay, life and death, and all other significant events are to his mind mysterious spiritual activities which are meant to manifest God's various designs. Of course the Oriental knows that except he plant the seed and properly care for it the blade, the ear, and the full corn in the ear will not grow. But he realizes also that it is not his planting and watering, nor the chemical and vital processes, but the World-Soul that giveth the increase. All other agencies are His tools. It was not so much the *ignoring* by the Oriental of the secondary causes, but their constant recognition *as such* which in the process of the centuries planted in the womb of his soul the seeds of holy books. He knew things and spoke of them in spiritual terms. God to him has been the center and synthesis of all things.

45

The Occidental, on the other hand, has not been satisfied with the contemplation of nature as the garment of an awful divine mystery. His quest has been and is to catalogue nature's doings and to know its self-running parts as a mechanic knows the parts of a clock. In his spiritual moments he reads the mystical Oriental scriptures which speak of childlike faith and the absorption of the soul in the Eternal. With exquisite cadence and nicety he reads those scrolls with all their naive, yet marvelous accounts of God's direct, manlike dealings with the human soul; but he reads with serious mental reservations. As yet his soul is divided in its allegiance between experimental science and mystical faith. His condescending admission and very consciously and nicely carved saying that "science and faith need not conflict with one another" has not yet become in him a welding medium of knowledge and faith. The word in him has not become flesh, and the immediate prospects do not inspire the hope of such incarnation.

For, to his great enchantment, the searching Occidental has found that it is gravitation, and not God, which guides the stars in their courses. Thermal changes bring about the wind and the rain and the lightning and the thunder, and not the Most High. Given so much nitrogen, so much phosphate, so much moisture and so much heat and light, and we have a good crop. "Planting in faith and watering in hope" may be good poetry, but it has no real bearing on an abundant, or meager harvest. And it is the urge of life in the seed, or the *elan vital*, and not God, which gives the increase.

No one can contemplate scientific research, so far as it goes, with anything but the highest regard. Yet the fact remains that the difference between gravitation and God as the power which maintains the stability of the heavens is in the end a spiritual one. The intellectual part here is the medium of approach. The real difference is to be found in the fact that contentment with secondary causes in our contemplation of nature may sow in us the seeds of encyclopaedias, but it cannot sow the seeds of scriptures. Not until the ultimate cause has absorbed in our minds all immediate causes and God has become all in all will the seeds of holy books begin to germinate in our nature.

But it may be pertinently asked here, "Is it not a fact that, because of his indifference to scientific research, the Oriental is very superstitious?" Broadly speaking this question must be answered in the affirmative. Yet the term "superstitious" is of relative significance. To those whom we call "hardheaded" persons everything in the realm of faith and imagination is superstitious. To such everything which cannot be apprehended by the senses, weighed and measured, is a superstition. To some faith in God is a superstition, to others patriotism is a superstition, still to others hero-worship, belief in immortality, and all sorts of invisible spiritual relations are superstitions. I imagine that if we could make a thorough and correct study of all grades of the human mind we should find in the end only one person - perhaps the most "hard-headed" - among men who is not superstitious, and that according to his own decree concerning, himself.

Yet, I do not wish to deny that the human mind does hold certain things to be real, which to experimental science are unreal, and that the Oriental has been and is in a measure captive of such notions. But the West is definitely committed to the acceptance of the great religious classics of the East as "holy scriptures." They are the chief source of its spiritual inspiration and the living flame on its altars. Now, when the Occidental calls the Oriental superstitious, would not the impetuous son of the East be likely to say to him, "Let me call your attention to the fact that the 'superstitions' of my people have been to your people the divine evidences of the reality and validity of the faith which is our common heritage. Remove from the scriptures all the elements which your scientists consider to be superstitious, and your divines would stigmatize the remaining portion as 'a mere code of morals.'"

It would indeed be very interesting to know what estimate a visitor from Mars would make of the comparative merits of the superstitious mind which produced the Bible, and the scientific mind which produced the poison gas, the submarine, and the eighteen-inch gun.

Of course, it goes without saying that superstitions or the ideas which do not represent reality are not fit to be the basis of religion or any other system of thought, and they never were. They represent a mode of operation which characterizes the human mind at a certain stage in its development and in its striving to apprehend reality. Their relation to rational faith is like that of childhood to maturity and of wild growth to the cultivated garden. As a rule cultivation is supposed to fulfill and not to destroy the life of the wild tree. The so-called modern mind overemphasizes the importance of demonstrable facts in their relation to the things men live by. It assumes a tremendous responsibility and runs in the teeth of history when it asserts that a superstitious mind is incapable of great achievements. Almost all the great moral and spiritual thoughts of history, all maxims of wisdom and words of consolation and spiritual peace, which alone are sought in life's most significant moments, whether in the palace or the hut, originated in those ages which are now called superstitious. Then man's conquests, victories, and gains were spiritual. His superstitions were the evidences, not so much of his fear of the unseen, but of his longing for spiritual self-fulfillment.

My own memories of the days of my childhood and youth, when I lived in such "scriptural atmosphere" of thought, do not seem to me to have been merely times of superstitious fear. The realization that God Himself was everywhere, "keeping watch over the evil and the good," gave the soul more security than fear. A great storm, an eclipse, a meteoric shower, or any other sublime natural phenomenon wore for us the aspect of a solemn high mass, rather than that of a hostile assault by the blind elements. God was in the awesome event. It was a grand symbolic performance by the Higher Power manifesting his glory and his might. Again let me say that it was such conceptions of natural events which laid the germs of the scriptures and the seeds of the church in the Oriental soul.

Now, what are the signs of the times? Is the production of a great spiritual literature impossible for such an age as the present? I think no one can be justified in shutting the door of hope by using the word "impossible" in this connection. Furthermore, I have much faith in America's youthful soul. To me this free-born nation has potentialities which are oceanic in their magnitude and strength. America has scarcely begun to realize her spiritual possibilities. Who can say what she might not accomplish if her mighty native forces are directed to spiritual ends and her young men and maidens led to see visions? But at present America is like a youthful giant who, while he has achieved many brilliant victories, has not as yet become fully conscious of his supreme mission in the world. So I am loath in this connection to speak of the production of a great spiritual literature as impossible. I should say, however, that it is impossible for a people to produce something like the Twenty-Third Psalm and the Thirteenth Chapter of First Corinthians, and the Standard Oil Company and the United States Steel Corporation, *at the same time.* In saying this I do not mean to pass judgment upon the moral status of such great enterprises. What I mean to say is that people often imagine that man has two sets of faculties, one with which to build great commercial and industrial enterprises, and the other to produce a great religious literature. This is a false conception. Personality is an indivisible unit. All its energies are at any given time guided by its supreme purpose. When this purpose is spiritual, man's faculties function spiritually; when it is commercial, the faculties function commercially, and so forth. With the same faculties we can worship God *or* Mammon, but we cannot worship both at the same time. When a people's overmastering desire is for spiritual greatness, although they may, as indeed they must, engage in commercial pursuits, their greatest men are bound to be prophets and seers, and not only financiers and engineers. In such a state of existence there is no need to subsidize a young man and promise him a pension for life in order to beguile him to enter a theological school and thus "recruit the ministry." Great prophets of religion are born, not only of their parents, but of the soul of their race. What a people sows that also shall it reap.

Chapter Ten - The Inner Sphere and the Outer Sphere

A GREAT cloud of witnesses, deep-visioned seers of all the ages, warn us never to forget that the real environment of the soul is a sphere within a sphere. The world of our physical senses - the outer sphere - is the field where man must labor. The world of spiritual contemplation - the inner sphere - is the city of God where man must live. These two worlds, supplementing each other, form man's universe and supply the needs of both the soul and the body. To the Hebrews the inner world was represented by the "secret place of the Most High," the holy of holies; to the Christians by a mystical union with Christ. Both doctrines mean the same thing, namely, being spiritually domiciled. Neither of these spheres is meant to take the place of the other. To neglect either of them is to live a one-sided, unbalanced life.

The Oriental may be said to have favored spiritual retreat too greatly, with the result that his material life has been so limited as finally to retard his progress, even spiritually. The Occidental, on the other hand, is certainly too much in the outer sphere. "The taming of nature," the exchange of numberless commodities, the camera, the motion picture, the ball game, the golf game, the daily newspaper with its hourly lurid "extras," the hideous advertising signs, the glaring lights, the automobile, and that balm for all manner of nervousness, the humorous story, keep him roaming over the surface of life.

The temple made with hands is no longer his soul-refreshing retreat. This keen-eyed toiler has rediscovered nature worship. He has rediscovered that "the groves were God's first temples," which the automobile renders very accessible. In those limitless temples he would "worship." So on the days which the much-criticized organized religion has set aside for religious observances, our modern man "takes to the woods." He is deeply enamoured of organization and concentration for efficiency in every other field but that of religion. He seeks nature; but with what companions, what intents and purposes, is no great matter.

Nature is a great inspirer, indeed, but she is such only for those who have the springs of inspiration within themselves. The "bush" burns, without being consumed, only for a Moses, for the man whose eye is furnished to see. A nook in the woods may be a temple for a spiritual mystic, or a den for one who is there in pursuit of unlawful pleasure. When the groves were God's first temples, man dwelt in caves, fed on raw flesh, was naked, and was not ashamed. The moral order has greatly changed since the cathedral has graced the earth with its sculptured beauty and majesty. Had the grove worship proved sufficient to guide man's moral and spiritual evolution, the cathedral never would have been raised.

Nature may provide us with much subjective pleasure. It can soothe our jaded nerves. It can awaken in the rightly tuned soul the sense of infinitude and transport it to realms of unspeakable peace. But nature does not rebuke us for our sins. It does not say to us, "Except ye be converted and become like little children, ye shall not enter into the kingdom of heaven." Its religion is a religion of release. It does not bring to our ears the cry of our oppressed fellow-beings. It does not say, "Go ye into all the world and preach the Gospel to all creation." It does not disturb our quietude with the solemn call of duty, "the stern daughter of the voice of God," nor does nature take up a collection.

As the groves are not quite fit to be financial institutions, nor chambers of commerce, nor colleges, nor homes for civilized men, so are they unfit as substitutes for churches.

The efforts that are being made in this country to-day by the churches (which, alas, are gradually coming to mean only the ministers), to reclaim and restore to religion the strayed millions, are in many instances highly commendable, but often very pathetic and indicate helplessness. Every sort of amusement is being dragged under the roof of the church building "in order to interest the men" in the most sacred issues of life. Somehow the means do not seem to fit the end. The preaching on the "issues of the day" does not seem to be of compelling interest to the business man, who as a rule knows more about those vexing issues than the minister does. Recently I read in the press that in a certain locality which is famous for its Sunday golf a wireless apparatus was to be installed for religious purposes. The lofty object of this enterprise is the transmission over this modern convenience of a "brief" sermon to the men so they can have their "little religious service" at the Golf Club without having it interfere too much with their play. "If the men do not come to the church, the church must go to them," was the exultant explanation of the originator of this device.

It is possible that such a reminder of the existence of God and man's duty toward Him might improve the language of those men while in action on the links. But what a pity it is to wrestle with God in prayer through a megaphone! What a pity it is that men of the twentieth century should substitute a club house for the sanctuary and the golf sticks for the candlesticks! No nation's soul can live and thrive and produce seers and holy books by feeding on such lunch-counter religion. How under such circumstances can one find life's holy of holies and meditate on "the law of the Lord "? Can any one imagine such a scattered, troubled, shallow life producing an Isaiah or a Paul? Here as everywhere the law of compensation works without a flaw. Great prophets of religion and the seeds of holy books are born of those who dwell in the mystic and untroubled soft light of the secret place of the Most High.

Chapter Eleven - The Grand Synthesis

I DO not wish to have it implied that I believe that the Occidental has completely lost sight of spiritual values. Far from it. He seems to me to be at present dazzled by his success in analyzing and classifying the modes of matter and life on the earth. By his success in this field he has been forced for the time being to *suspend* his mystical sense and devout spiritual aspiration, in the interest of objective knowledge. He does not sneer at faith in an overruling Providence. He is too dignified to do that. He simply suspends judgment until all the facts have been secured. He hopes some day to find out by searching whether, in placing himself and all his interests in the embrace of a gracious divine Providence, he is really in the everlasting arms, or simply operating psychologically on himself.

Nor does he willfully nor indolently subordinate the soul to its possessions. He is simply seeking to know whether the *soul really exists*. His experimental mind would know first whether this mysterious thing called "soul" is a stream of consciousness, a product of brain activity, an assembly of sensations, or a conscious spiritual entity capable of surviving the wreck of the body. Again, he would know whether so-called spiritual inspiration is the whispering of that resourceful sub-conscious self, which is "like unto a man that is an householder, which bringeth forth out of his treasure things new and old," or the evidence of fresh and awakening contact of the soul with God. The experimental psychologist and that new revelator the psycho-analysist, whose "complexes" are like the specialist deities of old, each one of whom presided over one or more of nature's forces and held the secrets thereof, are confidently expected to give correct answers to these weighty questions. The nerves and the muscles are being coaxed to give up their secrets and the digestive processes and the sexual instincts appealed to, to reveal their psychic mysteries.

It is not difficult to see then that through this ruthless analysis our great "modern thinker" has left no secret chamber in his soul as a dwelling-place for the spirit of prophecy. He has within him no spiritual ovarium for the seeds of holy books to germinate in. His soul is being torn asunder.

Now, the Oriental, the producer of scriptures, has for centuries held fast a simple synthetic philosophy of life essentially religious. His philosophy has not been broad -based, on wide and accurate scientific observations in the tangible world. To him this world is an adjunct to the inner world whose gates open toward the Infinite. Once set this inner world in order, and the outer world falls in in harmony with it. Seek first God's kingdom and righteousness, and all other desirable things shall be added to this supreme quest. So long as the Highest Good is accessible to the soul's vision, life's unity is secured by bending every effort in the direction of that Good and interpreting all events in terms of it. To the Easterner this sort of philosophy is the only study which is fully worthy of man; not the philosophy of things, but of spiritual being.

Through spiritual sympathy, intuition, and rational deduction, in view of the awesome wonders which the heavens and the earth spread before him the Oriental came into possession of the two central facts of being, God and the soul. As his knowledge widened his world was built around these two great facts. His scriptures have been the results of, first, his endeavor to establish the soul's conscious and harmonious relations with God. Second, to establish the reign of peace and love among men, not because they have all evolved from the same animal stock and have identical economic interests, but because they are children of God and brothers.

The truth of this unity of all things in God, the Easterner has had no reason these many centuries to question. Will the Westerner finally find a good reason to doubt this truth and to pronounce all things "vanity"?

I do not feel inclined to be so hopeless. At present, however, the advanced Western thinker is in his intensest analytical period. I love to think that he at least has the hope, elusive as that is, that by searching he may find God. At present this restless inquirer's laboratories are a great host. Specialization and dissection are his overmastering passions. The soul, the body, the mind, the Bible, as well as material substances, are being analyzed by him beyond recognition. Such words as "philosophy" and "theology" he looks upon with suspicion.

In a magazine article an English educator says: [1]

Men of to-day rarely call themselves philosophers, at most they describe themselves as devoted to one section of philosophy - logic, psychology, ethics, or metaphysics. Hence, philosophy, which ought to concern itself with the whole round of knowledge, the building up of the world of thought as a complete whole, commonly presents itself as a series of sectional studies, and by intense concentration on narrowed areas prides itself on producing an increasing number of mental sciences, approximating to the natural sciences. I suggest that the churches and philosophy ought to combine, or at least supplement each other in the promotion of the study of some synthetic philosophy of life...The philosophy that is wanted must be synthetic, presenting thought and life as wholes, not as further professional studies in the analytic and disruptive tendencies of isolated, separate, specialized sciences, however valuable those may be *in their* places.

There can be no doubt that at present the Western world is fostering the technical and commercial mind at the cost of the spiritual mind, and the analytical mind at the cost of the synthetic mind. Philosophy as a unifying, spiritual process of thinking is being neglected in the interest of experimental science. The polytechnic institutions are crammed with students, and the theological schools are only meagerly attended. The churches sadly reflect this state of things. Whether democracy will stand secure on such foundations remains to be seen.

The Occidental's achievements in the tangible world are full of grandeur, but it is the grandeur of promise of that which is yet to be. For until he has brought all his various interests into a grand spiritual synthesis, "presenting thought and life as wholes," he will remain a minor "under the law." His dealings will be only with partial and relative values. And when he has achieved this grand synthesis, he will find that his less scholarly Oriental cousin was not far wrong in his conclusions. He will find, as the Oriental has found, that ultimately the only thing of real value is religion and the only subject of permanent interest to the soul is God.

Notwithstanding the threatening dangers I have spoken of, I cannot allow myself to believe that this noble consummation is impossible to effect. Western civilization has by no means run its course in history. It is still intensely dynamic. It is not reasonable to believe that it will allow itself to be strangled spiritually in the flush of its youth.

The Occidental's analytical processes are the revealers of the deep mysteries of matter and life. They have enlarged the heavens and the earth far beyond any conception the Orientals ever had of them. His social sciences are establishing the sovereignty of personality, extending the bounds of human freedom, and knitting the nations together in the bond of mutuality. His industries are the whetstone of man's genius, tending constantly to increase and equalize the fruits of human endeavor. His educational systems compass all the spheres of his complex life and grip its manifold interests as gravitation grips all material objects. Great are his possessions and his powers! The super-eyes of his sciences have dazzlingly multiplied the number of the stars, reduced matter to an electric fluid, and placed in his hands stupendous forces. Shall such forces be allowed to turn upon him and rend him, or shall they be made stepping-stones to spiritual self-fulfillment? Shall they be allowed to lead him to the verge of the dark abyss of despairing agnosticism, or be so used by him as to reveal to him the ineffable light of spiritual reality? My faith in the latent possibilities of the Western mind lead me to believe that the latter shall be the case. When the mighty forces which science has placed in the Westerner's hands are put under the guidance of a spiritual purpose, and his democracy under the control of the spirit of human brotherhood, then, as the Easterner looked *from* nature to God, the Westerner will look *through* nature to God and find the unity of all things in Him. Then the martyrs of science will be placed upon the calendar of saints of the greater church of the future and the holy books of the East and the holy books of the West will together form the more inclusive scriptures of the race.

[1] Foster Watson, D.Litt., *The Hibbert Journal*, January, 1921.

Chapter Twelve - Industry Plus Life

IN the closing paragraph of Chapter I it was stated that the civilization of the Oriental rests on agriculture and religion, and the civilization of the Occidental on industry and education. The result of this has been that for many millenniums the Oriental has by thought and act maintained religion as the center of his individual and collective life, while with the Occidental, especially the Teuton and the Anglo-Saxon, religion is slowly becoming one of life's interests and is in danger of becoming one of life's minor interests.

Of course the Easterner is also an industrial worker and the Westerner an agriculturalist. The real difference between the two is a matter of emphasis. And here again the comparative presentation of the subject is not for the purpose of inviting the West to return to the rather primitive ways of the East, nor to invite the East literally to copy the methods of the West.

I am one of those who deeply regret the disappearance of the handcraftsman in any country. I deeply regret the crowding-out of existence by the standardized factory of the artisan's shop which bore its owner's name and reflected his personality. In that shop industry was life functioning freely and artistically on all its sides. The products of genius bore the stamp of the producer's soul. The customer grew into a friend, and the price of an article was felt by the seller to be a return of light to his mind and power to his body. Then there was a cordial intimacy between man and nature. The raw material stirred before the artisan's eyes with artistic possibilities, and the law of matter held sweet communion with the law of mind. Industrial artists created in town and city nooks and corners over which hung the mystical haze of romance. They themselves represented the productive vastness and ruggedness of the creative mind. Every stroke of their tools revealed the glory of the unseen and the latent beauty of the human soul. The truth and integrity of their minds, such as is reflected, for example, in old New England furniture, hallowed the work of their hands. They loved their labor, because it was an intellectual and moral exercise; it was of the nature of prayer in its spontaneity and dignity.

Then the customer was a connoisseur. He sought the artisan's wares as a lover. The desired article was to him a complement of his own personality. He sought the elegance of quality, and not the vulgarity of quantity; he *desired* the products of genius to live with, and not mere shining objects to display to the eyes of the curious. There were élite in those days. There was poetry in industry and deep and spiritual appreciation of its intensely human products. The hoard was small, but the heart was great.

I deeply regret the passing of that mode of life. And it is one of the significant signs of the times that the better minds among men to-day long for it as those who long for the morning. The very stupendous extent of the factory itself and its standardized products tend to create such longing. The seekers after hand-made articles to-day are not considered retrogressive, but artistic in taste.

Automatic machinery marks a new and great era in the history of man, but is making of men automatic machines. It is narrowing specialization to a point and rigidly standardizing human activities. The tender of an automatic machine may be a man, or a boy, a resourceful thinker, or one that acts as by instinct. He must by necessity conform to the law of the machine he tends and become identified with the particular piece which he handles. The inevitable vast consolidation of interests also is swallowing up the individual. As the operative is bound to be part of the machine he tends, so also is he bound to be a restricted unit of the labor union he joins. He is not free to own the tools with which he works, nor to fix his own wages, nor the number of his work hours.

But the pleader on the other side of this question cannot be ignored; he must be respectfully heard. He is willing to concede all that is said about the artistic charms, the dignity and substantial character of the products of the handcraftsman's genius. But his legitimate question is: "How many of the rank and file of the people in those 'good old days' did own and enjoy the products of the romantic shop?" His contention is that only a few could avail themselves of those elegant things. The élite were distinguished by their small number. There was an almost sheer drop from the elegance of the few to the shabbiness of the many. Handwoven silks and satins contrasted sharply with homespun fabrics. The ordinary man who was in the majority labored day and night to produce the few crude articles he used. The class line in the social world formed an insurmountable barrier. The life of the majority was greatly restricted. For being so limited materially, it was also limited intellectually. The handcraftsman in any field could not supply the market with his products at such prices as the common people could pay.

Now, contrast such conditions with those of the present time. Since the advent of the automatic machine life has broadened on all of its sides. The common man no longer looks with hungry eyes at the fine garments of the elite. A constant upward leveling both materially and intellectually is taking place in society. Social class distinctions can no longer be maintained as in the past. The department store is an equalizer of men, at least in appearance. The dollar does not buy so much as it did in the past, but we now have more dollars and more articles to buy with them. It is because of the automatic machine that the laboring man of to-day drinks his midday coffee while on the job out of a thermos bottle, carries a watch, reads a newspaper, and works only eight hours a day.

It would be sheer folly to undertake to dispute the truth of these assertions. The material comforts of life are immeasurably greater to-day than they ever were in human history. Those of us who feel inclined to mourn the fast disappearance of hand crafts must bear our sorrow patiently and accept the present order with the comforting thought that it has its compensations. The automatic machine is here, and here to stay and grow in extent and power. The stage-coach is gone, and the steam train is here, and perhaps soon the aeroplane will take the place of the train. The ox team is gone, and the motor plough is with us. It is not much use to long for "those days." It is our present selves and not our former selves that we have to think of.

Yes. And in drawing a contrast between the East and the West with regard to this phase of life, I do not mean in the least to belittle the industrial achievements of the civilization in which I find myself. My object is, first, to present the life of the East as it is, and, second, to ask whether the profound and beneficent changes in our material life are going hand in hand with equally profound and beneficent spiritual changes. There is a saying which is ascribed to Henry Thoreau (no matter whether correctly or not) which seems to me to be very applicable at this point. It is said that when that recluse of Walden Pond was asked whether he thought the steam train was better than the stage-coach, he answered, "Yes, if it carries better people; else it is only meanness going faster."

Perhaps it was because of ecstatic devotion to his dreams and visions that the Oriental has succeeded in setting bounds and limits to his inventive genius and, consequently, to his material wants. Throughout his long and significant history he has been a tool-user. He has known almost nothing of machinery. His own hands fashioned his tools for him, and the products of his simple industry have been manifestations, even extensions, of his personality. The foundation of his civilization has been agriculture. The thought of "the possible failure of the iron and coal deposits" has never invaded his mind or disturbed his repose. So long as the earth yields him food, and heaven visions, he feels that the strength of the hills is his.

Machinery with all it brings in its train has never existed for the son of the East to draw him away from his quiet, meditative life. His simple and intensely human occupations have always kept him in touch with his home, his church, and his friends. His little shop, and often his home, is his "factory." In that humble abode friendly intercourse goes hand in hand with labor. The shop is never so inviting as when the friends are there beguiling the hours with gossip, parable, and story.

Westerners often say that you never tire looking at a rug, a piece of embroidery, carved wood, or beaten brass of Oriental make. No, you never do. It is like looking at a waterfall, or a flower-dotted meadow. The fruits of the Oriental's labors are the fruits of his soul. In his handiwork centuries of domesticity and prayer are reflected. Patience, repose, skill, sorrow, laughter, are there, also. "In the name of God" he begins his task, and with "praise be to God" he ends it. He is never harried by "rush orders," nor lashed by the demands of the "merit system," nor distracted by the smell of factory oil and the growling whir of machinery. His leisurely labor is an extension of soul and transference of personality. This is why fine Oriental wares seem more like human companions than material possessions.

The Oriental has never classified pleasure and duty in a specialized sense and on the basis of priority. Pleasurable living has always been a duty with him, and duty that which at any given moment tended to make more singable the poetry of life. He works to live, and decidedly hates to think for a moment that he lives to work. The way in which storekeepers of my native town transacted business is one of the romantic memories of my youth. At times when I was sent on an errand to the chief store in the town I would find it closed. The storekeeper had guests on that day and he was at home entertaining them. The gain of trade was good, yet utterly insignificant when compared with the joy of having his friends gathered under his roof and around his table.

Thus, with no perpetual economic adjustments and readjustments to cram his life with vexing cares and problems, the son of the East has succeeded for these many centuries in maintaining religion as the center of his home and the simple social order in which he lives. For more than a hundred centuries his religious festivals have provided him with intellectual, social, and religious stimuli. His ruler has been to him a transient symbol of divine authority, the skilled worker an outlet of the divine mind, the educated man a repository of spiritual wisdom. The function of the learned man is not simply "to be fit to do something" in a technical or commercial sense, but to be "a guide to the blind, an instructor of the foolish, a teacher of babes."

The Occidental has been and is a man of many inventions. The forces of nature have become his tools. The genius of his education is revolutionary. Wherever he sets his foot he proceeds to change the face of the earth and to build, not on the ancient foundations, but according to his most recent vision of what ought to be. With him the past is forever forced forward. No sooner does he discover a law of nature than he uses it so as to compel nature to yield him more riches and power. He has objectified his knowledge in huge cities of a most complex life, in great and varied industries, and vast systems of transportation and communication. His inventive genius has placed in the centuries' line of succession the great "age of machinery." And machinery has relieved toil of much of its drudgery, made possible man's many brilliant victories over nature, on earth, sea, and in the air, revealed the hidden riches of the earth, greatly facilitated the diffusion of knowledge, brought the nations of the earth closer together and worked for physical cleanliness in home and city. So in place of the Oriental's slow-going camel, ox, and ass, the West has put the soulless, but lightning-like railway train, automobile, and airplane; in place of leisurely wielded hand tools, made still slower by the pleasant interruptions of visiting friends, the flashing shafts of machinery; instead of germ-infested homes and towns, a sterilized environment; instead of a few hand-written scrolls, hosts of finely printed books which no man can number; in place of dreams and visions, calculating intellectual alertness.

Certainly there is a vast difference between the Oriental mind and the Occidental mind. Compared with the latter the former seems decidedly primitive. The great achievements of the Occidental in the tangible world are dazzling, even to the passive Oriental. He also feels at first tempted to consider those achievements as the elements of true civilization. And well might he suspect that the Occidental has outdistanced him in the expansion of his mind and the enlargement of his personality.

Yet speculative argument as to which civilization is the better one, the Occidental or the Oriental, is of little value. The common ground of thought and deduction here is the fact which is accepted by both the East and the West, namely, that the real value of human life is to be found in its spiritual tendencies and achievements, and in no other. The progress of civilization must forever be measured, neither by tools nor by machinery, necessary as these may be, but by the greatness and perfectness of those agencies which tend to make the spiritual life lovable and attractive. When the achievements of the mind in the fields of education, industry, and commerce tend to make firmer the spiritual foundation of life, individual, domestic, and social, and enable men increasingly to give themselves to spiritual culture, then we have true civilization. Otherwise we have only big dividends; we are not growing better, we are simply going faster.

The Oriental, as I have already intimated, cannot escape being dazzled by the Occidental's great achievements. Nor does he consider them to be wholly and grossly materialistic. He sees in them a revelation of heroism, eagerness for knowledge, and a strong and deep passion for freedom, law, and order. Before such accomplishments the son of the East feels himself to be insignificant. He is led to believe that he has been asleep for these many centuries; that, while his submissiveness to the heavenly vision has been an unspeakable gain to him and to the world at large, his passive attitude toward this tangible world has been a decided loss. Yet a clearer view of the tumultuous activities of the aggressive Westerner gives the Easterner pause. He soon perceives that ceaseless battling with this material world, however heroic it may be, is not an unmixed blessing; that excessive aggressiveness, like its opposite, tends in the end to thwart its own purpose, and the will to conquer, unless its goal is spiritual, leads to defeat.

Chapter Thirteen - The Mandate of Business

THE Occidental is a man of many inventions, but with the increase of his inventions the center of his life is steadily shifting from the religious to the economic. With him intellectual alertness and commercial prudence are constantly gaining on the spirit of true piety. With no organized opposition to religion on his part, he is losing touch with it because his hands are full of other things. The upbuilding and perfecting of the agencies of true civilization - the home, the church, the school, and other spiritual institutions - are no longer his chief concern and his "meditation day and night." He has high regard for them but is too busy to serve them devotedly. The man, even in this country, which traditionally is neither indifferent nor opposed to the spiritual verities, is very little in the church, the home, and the school. *He is in business.* He is more ready to serve those great and indispensable institutions with his money than with his person. He has turned them over to the woman, and is in grave danger of the folly of believing in the possibility of a one-sex religion and a one-sex civilization. At present Business is the central word in his vocabulary. He even is strongly inclined to measure national greatness by the yield of the fields and the mines and the output of industry. Human skill, the schools, the government, the press, and what not exist to promote technical knowledge and business progress. International understandings must be promoted in order to prepare the way for more business, the League of Nations must be established for the purpose of "stabilizing international business," and even war and peace negotiations are being used by him as cataclysmic means for the opening of new markets and the greater extension of business.

In this great field I have profound admiration for the better type of the American business man. Here he is a hero, and I am a hero-worshiper. Whenever I meet him I love to study his face. There I find the evidences of courage, alertness, resolution. He is intelligent, quick to perceive, flexible, yet firm like tempered steel. He is richly endowed with initiative and deeply yearns for self-expression, full and free. The impulse of free America surges through his soul. Life to him is never a closed circle, but an open road to regions rich with discovery.

In his chosen field he enters the lists like a knight. With full consciousness, he faces great risks. He would win like a hero and, if need be, lose like a hero. He does not accumulate in order to hoard and toy with his wealth. He makes millions, and he gives millions. His enchanter is not so much wealth as achievement. He is neither mean nor sordid; neither a sneak nor a bully, but fights like a true soldier in the open field. His love of power as a producer far exceeds his love of mere money. He is keenly conscious of his individualism and unalterably opposed to its curtailment. He is free-born and as such unembarrassed by the consciousness of hereditary autocracy or aristocracy. His word is "forward." His assets of wealth and power are his pride because they are his achievements.

This is the better type of business man in America and he is magnificent in the business world he has built. This is the type from which has come such men as William Henry Baldwin, Jr., Henry Lee Higginson, Henry Pomeroy Davison, and many others, men to whom business, nay, life itself, was a sacred trust to be spent in the ministry of civilization. What a happy world this would be if all business men viewed life from such a standpoint!

Yet, the fact cannot be ignored that to millions of men in this country life is only business in the narrowest sense of the term. The factory and the market are the two poles of their world. Idealism to them is a haze of fancy. It is good for the preacher, the Sunday-School teacher, and the entertaining after-dinner speaker. In business, however, it is a thing which tends to weaken the fiber of life and soften the brain. Here hardheadedness and unremitting toil are power and security. Such men possess to a great extent the ability of the nobler type of the business man just mentioned, minus his vision of life. They are quick-witted, strong and brave, but are uncomfortably suspicious of rivals and lack faith in the spiritual destiny of their country and the world at large. They are inconsiderate opportunists. Their creed seems to be, "Each man for himself, and let the devil take the hindmost." On business subjects, as they understand business, they talk like men; on ethical and religious subjects, they talk like children. They tell you with distressing frankness that such things are not in their line.

It is such men, who seem to make up the majority in the commercial world of to-day, who give the Easterner an unfavorable impression of Western civilization. It is because of this type of mind that the high admiration on the part of the Oriental for the achievements of the Occidental mind is sobered. He sees that the Westerner's fine, systematic, intellectual and industrial progress has far outdistanced his spiritual progress. He says to him, "Come, let us reason together. You call your thousand material devices 'labor-saving machinery,' yet you are forever 'busy.' With the multiplying of your machinery you grow increasingly fatigued, anxious, nervous, dissatisfied. Whatever you have, you want more; and wherever you are, you want to go somewhere else. You have a machine to dig the raw material out of the ground for you, a machine to manufacture that raw material into various articles for you, a machine to transport the articles, a machine to sweep and dust, one to carry messages, one to write, one to talk, one to sing, one to play at the theater, one to vote, one to sew, another to keep things cold, another to keep things hot, another to beat the egg, and a hundred others to do a hundred other things for you, and still you are the most nervously busy man in the world. You have very little, if any, time for spiritual culture. Your haunts are not the home, the church, the literary circle, the civic forum, but the store, the office, the factory, and the business men's club. Your devices are neither time-saving nor soul-saving machinery. They are so many sharp spurs which urge you on to invent more machinery and to do more business."

I think there is much truth in the foregoing observations. The Westerner has not been using machinery simply and purely to relieve life of its drudgery and give the surplus time thus created to other than material pursuits. Recently an American lady said to me: "Why do you speak against machinery - or at any rate the present use of it? It took my grandmother five hours to do by hand the sewing which I now do in one hour on the sewing machine." "Yes, madam," I replied. "But what do you do in the other four hours?" "More sewing," she answered, with a sweet smile. In this phrase we have the key to the whole situation. Every machine invented not only claims more of our time for its use and maintenance, but inevitably leads to the creation of another and faster machine. And with this increase the seat of power shifts from man as the controller of the machine to the machine as the controller of man. He *must* keep up with the impersonal, implacable force he sets in motion, and, as a consequence, neglect spiritual pursuits. The Westerner is at present in that situation. With him economic interests take precedence over all others.

One of the most striking evidences of this state of mind is a book by Thomas Nixon Carver, Professor of Political Economy at Harvard University, entitled, "The Religion Worth Having." [1] To this noted economist the best religion is that "which (1) acts most powerfully as a spur to energy, and (2) directs that energy most productively. That is the most productive expenditure of energy which supports the most life and supports it most abundantly, which gives the largest control over the forces of nature and the most complete dominion over the world, and which enables men to control whatever environment happens to surround them and to live comfortably in it." This is the Alpha and the Omega of this little volume. Its three dominant words are "energy," "efficiency," "productivity." Only the religion that enables man to exercise economic control over the earth will live; all other religions and their adherents are inevitably doomed. Religious fervor is good only in so far as it can be harnessed as an economically productive power. The aesthetic and subjective enjoyment of religion is an unlawful indulgence; it is "pigtrough philosophy."

"The end of production," says Professor Carver, "is further production...we should consume in order that we might produce...if we have more energy than is necessary to sustain life the surplus should be used for further productive achievement...and an extension of our dominion over the world."

The altogether dispensable doctrine that "we should consume in order that we might produce," and, conversely, of course, that we should produce in order that we might consume, and own more of the earth's surface in order that we might produce more and consume more, reminds one of a certain prayer. An enterprising old farmer is said to have prayed, "O Lord, send more rain, to raise more corn, to feed more cattle, to buy more land to raise more corn."

This may be good economics, but, I think, it is poor appraisal of spiritual values. Its message is quite unnecessary in an age whose passion for "production" and economic conquest approaches madness. It is like the cracking of a whip over the head of a horse that is already running at top speed. Even the ancients knew the professor's thesis, but *they* appreciated at least its futility. The "certain rich man" in the Gospel parable, who pulled down his barns and built greater, and who "grew not from character to character, but from barn to barn," knew the philosophy of this "religion of productivity." But, when he was asked by the Spirit of the higher life what it was all for, he had no answer to give. We do not need to call upon religion to furnish the energy for production and more production; the necessities of life and selfishness and greed are amply sufficient to achieve that end. Production and more production, and the rivalries between the "producing" nations in the last fifty years to own the world came very nearly wiping their civilization out completely. It seemed for a time that only the quietists - the "pig-trough" philosophers - would be left to inherit the earth.

The theory that "if we have more energy than is necessary to sustain life the surplus should be used for further production" is the vogue in the modern world to-day. But there is not one of the great spiritual seers, poets, and romancers of history who deems this theory a worthy ideal for mankind to pursue. Industry is indeed commended by all the great religions as honorable, but only so far as it is needed "to sustain life," and not as an end in itself. This need having been supplied, men must then direct the surplus energy to the production of spiritual literature, poetry, art, and give themselves to the *aesthetic and subjective enjoyment of these things* to the end that they may bear the fruit of "love, joy, peace, longsuffering, gentleness, goodness, faith, meekness, self-control."

Material progress is not unworthy to be admired, and the ministering to physical well-being is a duty which cannot be safely and honorably neglected. But that progress which feasts the acquisitive and combative faculties and starves the religious and altruistic is false. It is commercial and industrial, but it is not human. To idealize it is to confuse values and to make the soul the bond-servant of the body. It is this one-sided progress which is threatening the present civilization with a thousand dangers and drying up its spiritual springs. Through our many inventions we have so multiplied the material things we use as to spend almost all our time exchanging them and building fleets and organizing armies to defend them. I feel certain that if America's spiritual progress had kept pace with its material progress it would be to-day a Zion upper-room fraternity without a Judas and an Eden without a serpent. I think the moral value of such books as the one mentioned above is to be found in the evidence they give as to the seed which the uncontrolled striving for economic power and dominion is sowing in men's minds. Volumes of statistics are crowding out the prophetic scrolls and the anxiety to make a living is killing the art of making a life.

I am not hopeless of the future. Yet of one thing I am firmly convinced. Up to the present the evidence is very clear that religion and machinery do not go together. Thus far the factory refuses to be the handmaiden of the church. The present fondness for machinery is a juvenile characteristic. It tends to engender wonderment rather than idealism, curiosity as to what strange things the machine will do next, rather than the desire to convert material into spiritual forces. Man cannot idealize a machine without worshiping a thing that is lower than himself. Again, machinery multiplies labor, calls for constant and thorough intellectual specialization, increases indefinitely man's material wants, and thus makes the struggle for economic existence so severe as to leave no time for spiritual development. The allurements of the "job" in the industrial centers, with its "ready money," constantly tend to increase the urban and decrease the rural population, with the inevitable result that, as the consumers of the food necessaries of life increase, the producers of those necessaries decrease. This is having its direful effect, not only in America, but in other countries. Emigration to the industrial centers of America is starving agriculture in the Old World. With this the stupendous problems of "capital and labor" grow more intricate and more vexing.

Through this rapid regrouping of populations in the West, society is compelled to devote the major part of the time and attention it can spare from business to three things: food, shelter, sanitation. These are the "issues of the day" and the elements of the "social gospel." The church which does not devote itself to these problems is stigmatized as an "old-fashioned, backward-looking institution." The church is no longer expected by the multitude to be purely a "house of prayer for all people," a shrine where the individual may seek the pure heart and the right spirit and where he is led to experience a new birth by the power of Him who makes all things new. No; the preference of the time is that the church should be a sort of forum where "practical religion" - that is, the religion of food, shelter, and sanitation - may be vigorously discussed. The minister must not be "too introspective." He must be a leader in the community advocating clean streets, pure milk, better housing "for the poor," and other essential necessities.

Of course, the church cannot disregard its environment. It must serve the social order in which it exists, *but without dissolving into the surrounding atmosphere.* At present the church is in grave danger of becoming the docile, obedient handmaiden of the factory. It is in danger of being compelled to "serve tables," or become an alien to the spirit of the age.

Is there not in this age of all sorts of specialists a place for the spiritual specialist? Are we to magnify the office of a specialist in every other field excepting that of religion? Is the medical specialist, the surgical specialist, the nerve specialist, the financial specialist, and every other kind of specialist, to be considered great, but the religious specialist to be stigmatized as narrow-minded? Is there no room in the present social order for a soul specialist as for the manicurist and the hairdresser, or do we not have any soul? Is there to be no place in this world where one may retire from the din and noise of this feverish life and for the moment forget its clashing material interests and seek to put his soul in tune with the Soul of all being? A place where a bruised heart can be healed, a stained conscience cleansed, a weak moral purpose strengthened, and a sin-enslaved soul set free?

It is never safe to indict a whole social order. Yet that social order which consents to having the fire of its religious altar sink into a flicker indicts itself. The ministry of religion to-day does not occupy the commanding position in the minds of men it deserves to occupy. The minister of religion, instead of being required to be an efficient spiritual specialist, is expected to be a little of everything, and "such a fine fellow that you wouldn't know he was a parson." The demand of the people is creating its own supply.

It is true that religion cannot be, like medicine and dentistry, restricted to a sharply defined field, but must embrace all the affairs of life. Yes, religion must be all-embracing, but it must first be *religion* before it can be so inclusive. It can be all-embracing only when it is able to command the allegiance of the soul as an undisputed divine mandate, and in no other way. Once let it assume this sway over the souls of men and it will embrace all their affairs.

But I am aware of the fact that this estimate of present conditions in the West, especially in America, would seem one-sided and tinged with willful ignorance if I should fail to speak of the mighty wave of idealism which swept this country during the World War. That remarkable phenomenon has been considered a decisive evidence that American civilization is not sordidly materialistic. This is very true. And I further assert that even without that thrilling evidence no intelligent and just observer could have called American civilization sordidly materialistic. The noble enthusiasm of the war *revealed* the latent idealism of America, and did not create it out of nothing. The pure flame of patriotism which lighted this country during that period not only makes every one of us who witnessed it forever proud of his American citizenship, but will light the paths of the unborn generations to duty and sacrifice.

Nevertheless, war idealism can be said to be the exclusive possession of no one people. Nor is it necessarily the evidence of the highest state of civilization. When a man realizes that his home is being attacked, be he a vicious gambler or a good, public-spirited citizen, if he is not infirm or an abject coward, he will give himself unreservedly to the defense of his home. What the Americans and the British and the French did during the war in defense of their democratic institutions the Germans also did in defense of their imperialistic institutions and the Turks in defense of their Califate. They also, after they had been made to believe that they were being attacked, placed their all on the altar of their country and fought for it with great heroism.

It is immeasurably easier to be an idealist and to look with contempt on material gain when the battle-flags are unfurled and martial music thrills the air than in prosaic times of peace. And it may not be out of place to say here that there is rarely a people which after a war escapes discreditable reaction from such idealistic enthusiasm.

My criticism of Western civilization is by no means a cry of despair. Its latent forces are still great and vital. Its youth is not all behind it. It is still capable of dreaming beautiful dreams and seeing noble visions. But at present it has reached a stage of threatening material prosperity and is swaying and straining under the immense weight of its external machinery. Its body has grown so huge that it is in danger of going beyond the control of its soul.

The inescapable fact is that religion - true, spiritual religion, and not only the "social gospel" - and machinery must go together if Western civilization is to endure. It is neither possible nor, indeed, desirable that the West should go back to the too simple life of the East. But the great imperative which cannot be safely ignored is that as the East has for centuries maintained religion as the center of its simple life, the West also must maintain religion as the center of its complex life or suffer defeat. So far in history God has been a God of agriculture. The Oriental has reared to Him altars in every field and offered to Him the first fruits of every season. Will the Occidental succeed in making God a God of industry and rear an altar for Him in every industrial center? This I consider to be the paramount "issue of the day" and the supreme challenge to Western civilization.

[1] *The Religion Worth Having.* (Houghton Mifflin Company, Boston.)

Chapter Fourteen - A "Working" Leisure Class

THE word "ease" which is so agreeable to the East has become rather disreputable in the Western world. It seems to the Anglo-Saxon as unnatural as the word "meekness." It is so difficult for this man of conquest to see how an easy-going people can subdue the earth and how the meek ever can inherit it.

He thinks that he finds the key to the Oriental mind in a passage in the Bible story of the creation. He finds that, in order to account for the disagreeable fact that he had to work in order to live, the Oriental asserts in that passage that it was all because he sinned at the beginning of human existence and as a result was doomed to work. "Because thou hast hearkened unto the voice of thy wife," says the Bible, "and hast eaten of the tree, of which I commanded thee, saying, Thou shalt not eat of it: cursed is the ground for thy sake; *in toil* shalt thou eat of it all the days of thy life." In this passage the aggressive Occidental finds the sum and substance of the Oriental's philosophy of labor. This ancient theory seems to him to have governed the Oriental's life throughout the centuries. And although the evidence is not perfectly clear that labor is a real joy and delight to the masses of the West to-day, nevertheless Occidentals have no patience with the "lazy" Oriental.

With a slight twisting of the real facts this accusation of the son of the East may be accepted as just. He is not desperately in love with constant toil, not because he thinks it a curse, resulting from an ancient sin, but because to him it is sin itself. To give so much of his time and effort to labor and the cravings of the flesh does not harmonize with his basic belief that this life is only a pilgrimage and a temporary stopping place on the way to eternity.

The Westerner cannot be and should not be like the Oriental. Lack of activity does not necessarily mean devotion to spiritual ideals. It may induce meaningless brooding, loafing, and all other harmful things that come with it. "Idleness is corrosive. Human energies, like human stomachs, turn inward perversely and self-destructively if they have not material to work on. Deprived of work, people exhaust themselves like crazed animals beating against their bars, even when the cage is of their own making. Thoughts, that should run out in path-finding, path-making labor, circle round and round within the mind, till it is dizzy and all distinctions are blurred. By work you straighten out such cramped and twisted energies, as you shake a reefed sail." [1]

The Orientals would do well, indeed, to heed the advice of this Occidental philosopher.

A vice is never anything else but a misused virtue; it is the unlawful use of our normal desires and faculties. The alternation of work and rest in the life of a man is an obvious necessity. It is excessive indulgence in either direction which stamps him either lazy or a ceaseless toiler. In respect of this phase of life the Oriental and the Occidental view one another from two extremes. The one seems as sluggish as a drone; the other as frenzied as a hornet. The Oriental seems to be weighted with the inertia of centuries; the Occidental to be violently driven by all the liberated forces of a scientific age. It is very difficult for either one sympathetically to understand the other. There seems to be no common ground for such an understanding. The flow of the West into the East is due in no small degree to this difference in velocity, both mental and physical.

It is not possible by argument to convince the Occidental that the Oriental is not so lazy as he seems, and it may be safer in any case to say that he is not so active as the modern age requires that he should be. Nor would it pass unnoticed, even if it were honest, to beg the question by saying that his mode of living does not require such strenuous activities. The common man in the East has been an agricultural laborer and trade worker since Adam's time.

From the very nature of the case his labor has been less hard and exacting than modern industrial labor. His daily fare has been frugal, but he has always earned his bread by the sweat of his brow. What has given the East its reputation for laziness has been its aristocrats rather than its common people. This class of men bears this reputation in almost every country. In the West, however, its status has undergone greater changes than in the East. Yet, even in the West, the socialists and their allies assert that by virtue of the present industrial system a new aristocratic class, which lives and gathers wealth by the sweat of the "toiling masses," is being formed in this country. Large dividends, high prices, and small wages, it is claimed, are responsible for this objectionable classification of the people. The study of this phase of our modern life, however, falls outside the scope and purpose of the present work.

Here I wish to call attention to a "working" leisure class which to my mind has been the real nobility of the East. It is that class of men whom I knew and revered as a youth and for whom the experiences of many years in the Western world have not lessened my regard. In almost every village and town in the East is found a group of landowners and merchants in whose lives work and leisure alternate in a very happy manner. They work in the fields and vineyards with their hired men, whom they equitably compensate, without forgetting their domestic and public obligations. They live with their children and endeavor to bring them up after the noblest traditions of their homeland. They are given to hospitality in person, and not by proxy. They give a certain portion of each day or certain days of each week to their assembling together for social intercourse and for the discussion and service of public interests. They are dignifiedly attired, the wealthier of them in Damascus silks, Persian *keshmir,* and European broadcloth. They are chaste of speech and of dignified bearing. They concern themselves with such matters of government as their rulers leave to them, such as the allotment of the local taxes, the appointment of watchmen for the vineyards, and other minor but important services. They represent their town at public gatherings in other towns, such as funerals and weddings, which are generally made municipal events. They are sought for advice in matrimonial matters, in the determination of property values, and kindred concerns of their humbler fellow-townsmen. They admonish the unruly, compose differences, which otherwise might lead to litigation, and faithfully serve their religious institutions.

My memory of such men, even in that simple social order, is to me one of the most precious elements of my inheritance. It is a lifting ideal which no changes in time and place can take away from me. It is enough for any man to possess such a vision of life. To those men gain was precious, but never so precious, never so satisfying as a good life put at the service of the community. To be a good, useful, God-fearing citizen was to them life's supreme ideal.

America is by no means impoverished in this respect. Public-spirited citizens are to be found in every community, especially as "givers" to good causes. But, when we take into consideration its wealth and intelligence as compared with the less progressive East, we are compelled to admit that such men are nowhere nearly so numerous in American society as they should be. Is the aim of progress to give us the business man to whom business is an end in itself, or the man to whom business is a means to serve the moral and spiritual interests of the community? As wealth accumulates, are men to decay? America needs to-day a "working" leisure class, whose activities shall be inspired by love of country and love of fellow-men, and not only of achieving in an economic sense. Business is excellent as servant, but is very tyrannical as master. Millions of money do not necessarily mean power; they may be a source of weakness and evil. The American business man must train himself in some way to know when he has achieved enough and had enough to maintain a decent standard of living with its *elevating* luxuries, when to let go doing for self and for "the maintenance of the business," and give himself, when he can still be useful, to the service of the public good.

Upon his retirement from business, Mr. Edward Bok, former editor of the "Ladies' Home Journal," had this to say:

One of the most pathetic sights in our American business life is the inability of men to let go, not only for their own good, but to give the younger men behind them a chance. They hang on beyond their years of greatest usefulness and efficiency; convince themselves that they are indispensable to their business, while, in scores of cases, the truth is exactly the opposite; the business would be distinctly benefited by their retirement and the resultant coming to the front of the younger blood in affairs...The real trouble with the American business man is that in many instances he is actually afraid to let go because, out of business, he would not know what to do. For years he has so immersed himself in business, to the exclusion of all other interests, that at fifty or seventy he finds himself a slave to his business, with positively no inner resources...A man must unquestionably prepare years ahead for his retirement. I do not mean alone financially, which naturally is paramount, but mentally as well. I have been interested to note that in nearly every case where a business man has told me that I have made a mistake in my retirement, and that the proper life for a man is to stick to the game and see it through...it has been a man with no resource outside of his business. Naturally, my action is a mistake in the eyes of such a man; but think of the pathos of such a position, where, in a world of so much interest and an age so fascinatingly full of worthwhile things, a man has allowed himself to become so absorbed in business that he has become a slave to it and to it alone, and cannot imagine another man happy without the same bone at which to gnaw. [2]

Mr. Bok himself is a striking illustration of the theory of life he champions. He has been able to make the transition from work as a private enterprise to work as a public service so easily because his business in life was saturated with humanitarian ideas. He apparently never allowed himself to forget during his years of business endeavor that he was a man first, and a business man afterwards. He kept company with the spiritual producers of history, remained in close touch with the American home, kept his sympathies open to humanitarian causes, and knew patriotism in terms of character and service. He spoke from experience when he said, "A man must unquestionably prepare years ahead for his retirement." Great accomplishments always have a long history. The business man I have described in the preceding chapter talks about business like a man, and about ethics and religion and spiritual culture in general like a child, because of his long preparation for and devotion to the one phase of life, and his neglect of the other. That is why he would feel "lost" if he should let go of his business.

There ought to be in every American community a building or a temple reared and dedicated to humanitarian culture. It should be whenever possible a marble palace of great beauty and sublimity fit to represent a nation's cultural, civic, and philanthropic ideals: a temple to which the citizens, regardless of party or creed, should come at short and stated intervals, not for the purpose of listening to the "ticker" of the stock exchange, nor to read the market quotations, nor to discuss foreign credits, but to commune with the great poets and romancers of all the ages, to receive the inspiration of art and music, to discuss civic interests which have no bearing on party politics, but are human concerns, to discover the spiritual side of citizenship, and to foster every other influence which tends to produce the free, beneficently intelligent and cooperative citizen. The churches might be made to do all this if we had one form of religion for all. But this, however desirable it might seem to many, is not yet possible. Let the temple of humanitarian culture supplement the work of the various churches and educational institutions, as the means of a higher unity which shall in process of time soften existing prejudices and put every man above his creed in the sight of his fellow-men.

Why should a business man allow himself to lose touch with the great literary and religious treasures of history? In them there is life. The dividend which the investment of such wealth in one's life yields is that very power which is needed to enable a business man to let go of his private business and give himself to the larger service of the community, without feeling "like a fish out of water." And what if devotion to these ends did not enable us to do so much business as we are now doing? Great wealth is desirable, but it does not seem to yield a corresponding increase of human happiness. Beyond a certain point, which seems difficult to indicate, it becomes rather a liability than an asset. In the last analysis the wealth of nations is neither gold nor silver nor institutions, but men and women whose type of culture is such as to enable them to trust, idealize, and love one another. We can understand wealth and civilization itself to be real only in terms of human excellence.

It seems to me that in his "symphony" William Henry Channing, a wise man from the West, gave a fine charter for the life of a true gentleman. He says:

To live content with small means; to seek elegance rather than luxury, and refinement rather than fashion; to be worthy, not respectable; and wealthy, not rich; to study hard, think quietly, talk gently, act frankly; to listen to stars and buds, to babes and sages, with open heart; to bear all cheerfully, do all bravely,

68

await occasions, hurry never; in a word, to let the spiritual, unbidden and unconscious, grow up through the common: This is my symphony.

Perhaps the precepts in this symphony which will seem easiest for the Easterner, but hardest for the Westerner to follow, are, "to live content with small means," and to "hurry never."

True, the environment of the American business man is vastly different from that of the Oriental. The many complexities of life in the West make the Oriental's life seem extremely simple. Yet the moral problems of this highly complex life are correspondingly great. If the business interests in the West demand the services of greater men than the Eastern landowners and traders, so also the attendant moral problems require spiritual heroes to grapple with them. If, as the growth of his influence seems to indicate, the business man is to be the leading man of the future, what preparation is he making for such a position? What faculties is he developing to deal with the problems of government, good citizenship, education for civilization, the security and purity of the home, the spiritual leadership of the youth, and the general elevation of the moral tone of society at large? Proxies do not work here. Money contributions and passive sympathy are entirely inadequate. Machinery is no sure guaranty of integrity, purity, and fair play. The problems of life of any sort are in the end moral problems and can be solved only by men and women who, in addition to their intellectual skill, are morally great.

The East has never allowed itself to lose sight of this basic fact. To it, above all things, "righteousness exalteth a nation." The West can no longer safely presume to substitute for this exalting power vocational education, mechanical skill, and the vast production and distribution of commodities.

The East, on the other hand, can no longer safely presume to stand still, as it has done for so many centuries. Its soul must function through a larger and more complex body than it has had heretofore. The aggressive, revolutionary genius of the West has radically changed the conditions of life in its own realms and is rapidly affecting other peoples. The East can no longer remain irresponsive to the action of the new leaven. The only question here is, How shall the renewal of the life of that Old World be effected? Shall the West swallow up the East and obliterate its distinctive characteristics? Even if that were possible, it would be an irreparable loss to the world. The world needs a characteristic Oriental civilization as it needs a characteristic Occidental civilization. That colorful, poetical Oriental type of life must not be utterly destroyed. Yet the West cannot fundamentally change the soul of the East without causing such destruction. On this the imperialistic colonizers seem to be bent.

The remaining chapters of this volume will be devoted to the consideration of this phase of our subject.

[1] *What Men Live By*, page 13, by Richard C. Cabot, M. D.
[2] "Just Because I Want to Play," the *Atlantic Monthly*, September, 1920.

Part Three - Points of Contact between the East and the West

Chapter Fifteen - Invasions, Ancient and Modern

ASIA and Europe have had intercourse with each other ever since the beginning of European history. From the time when those tribes and nations of Asiatic origin began their westward march in remote antiquity, and laid the foundations of European society, to the present, the East and West have not lost touch with one another. Military conquests, commerce, travel, educational interests, and religious pilgrimages have been the points of contact between those two worlds.

It was very natural that the first flow of the tide of conquest should have been from the East into the West. The more ancient world pressed toward its recent offspring as by the power of gravitation. It was in the normal course of human events that the enterprising and highly civilized Phoenician should have planted his trade colonies on the eastern shores of Europe, and for the warrior tribes of Asia to have pushed their conquests to the very heart of that continent. The later Asiatic invasions of Europe, as the more recent European invasions of Asia, have all followed the same course.

The Persians, the Huns, the Avars, the Mongols, the Arabs, the Saracens, the Turks, and others, carried on vast military operations against Europe for centuries. Through these conquests intellectual and moral influences flowed from Asia into Europe. Chief among these by-products of military conquests were the great educational influences exerted upon mediaeval Europe by the Arabs in Spain, who stood for a long period as the custodians of culture west of the Mediterranean. But the greatest moral force with which Asia invaded Europe without sword or spear was Christianity. This Eastern-born religion found its way into Europe at a time of serious moral and religious disorganization, as a current of fresh life poured into a dying world. How profoundly this faith affected the life of Europe in the early stages of its development is impossible to state. The collective response of human society to the appeal of spiritual ideals is very slow, and the recent history of Europe would make it seem that the transformations which Christianity has effected in the lives of the European nations have not been so profound and revolutionary as believers in the great potency of this faith think they have been. Yet it would be utterly unreasonable to believe that the Christian Church, with its living faith, its art, its scholarship, and its philanthropy, has failed during these many centuries to impress itself beneficently upon the mind of Europe. Bad as Europe has been with the Church in its midst, it is safe to say that it would have been much worse without it.

The European invasions of Asia have been as natural to humanity as the Asiatic invasions of Europe. The causes in both cases were about the same. In either case, the military conqueror, the merchant, and the missionary responded to the urge of ambition and the beckoning of opportunity.

The first invasion of the East by the West was successfully undertaken by Alexander of Macedon. The armies of the great conqueror marched unbeaten from Macedonia to India. Rome followed Alexander with a slower pace, but with a more permanent organization. "With a Roman body and a Greek soul" her Empire embraced a large portion of Asia, and there seemed to be no reason why it should not endure forever. Joined to other agencies, the Arabs and the Turks crushed the Romans and ruled in their place. The Crusades formed the third invasion of the East by the West. The armies of the Cross fought against the armies of the Crescent. Undisciplined fanaticism battled against undisciplined fanaticism in. what seemed to be religion's age of childhood. In the course of time the knights of Europe and their picturesque armies returned (those of them who did) to their respective countries much wiser than when they set out on their sacred mission.

All those great conquests began and ended, and the ancient East remained the same mysterious, inscrutable world it was before Greece and Rome and Christian knighthood came into being.

In more recent times, the Dutch, the English, the French, and the Russians have been the chief invaders of Asia. Into that ancient continent, the mother of prophets and sages, these invaders have gone as warriors, merchants, educators, and missionaries. In one way or another they now exercise authority over about half of the one billion Asiatics. Their modern ideas, variously represented in educational institutions, laws, machinery, and merchandise, are impinging themselves upon the vast and deep life of the hoary East much like the clingers of a vine press against the body of a mighty oak.

The intents and purposes of these modern invaders of "lethargic" Asia are by no means all selfish and cruel. Even among the diplomats and the merchants that continent has friends. Their entrance into Asia has not been always effected by the sword. The English confess that in many cases they found themselves (as in the case of India and Egypt) compelled to assume the responsibility of rulers, much against their own original intentions. When they first went into India as simple traders, they found that country in a state of "anarchy." It was not a safe place to live in, much less to do profitable business. In fact it was Destiny, or Fate, or whatever it was, which made it a moral obligation for them to pacify and unite that unhappy Eastern country. The widening of their conquests in India had, as they confess, no other purpose. It was to make it safe for commerce for "all nations." The Hindus as a general rule could not view the situation from that standpoint, but it was all due to their incapacity to see such things in their true light.

71

So also it was in the case of Egypt. In 1882 there was a nationalistic rebellion in that country which jeopardized the lives and interests of Europeans. The Khedive proved unable to put down the uprising. England called upon the interested European Powers to take joint action with her in pacifying the country. The other Powers were not quick enough to respond. France indicated her willingness to cooperate, but failed to do so at the right moment. Both a British and a French squadron were in the harbor of Alexandria during the disturbance. But the French admiral, lacking orders to act, left for Port Said; so the British admiral was left all alone. Again it was Destiny, or Fate, which placed England in a critical position. The British admiral *had* to act in order to save the situation, and so he did act magnificently. The British entered Egypt, and the "turbulent" state of the country compelled them to stay in it for so many years in order to save it from anarchy. It would seem that the English never went forth seeking an empire, but that the empire which they now control in some unaccountable way fell into their hands.

The French could tell a somewhat similar story with regard to their colonial possessions. There was always some disturbance, some trifling with the rights and privileges of Europeans, which compelled European intervention and occupation of Eastern countries. The partitioning of China, it is asserted, was done for China's own good and the good of Asia in general. It was apparently for this reason that France annexed Cochin China and Tonquin, Russia appropriated Manchuria as a sphere of influence, Germany seized Tsing-Tau and Kiau Chau, and England laid her hand on Wei-Hai-Wei as a naval base. The French, who have recently gone into Syria against the will of the vast majority of its people, have repeatedly declared that, having been for centuries the protectors of the Christians in that country, they now deem it their solemn duty to occupy Syria and see to it that it has a good and stable government. Now they say they are ready to evacuate the country as soon as a stable native government is established in it, again they assert that they are there to stay forever.

But this conception of duty toward the native populations involves still another matter. Each one of the colonizing Powers is not only conscious of such a duty, but is even more keenly aware of the fact that it must not willingly permit any one of the other Powers to supplant it in its own coveted sphere of influence and discharge that high moral obligation in its place. The diplomatic scales must not be allowed to be tipped in favor of a rival colonizer. When I said to a French diplomat in Paris, "Your giving up of your old claim to Syria would mean no great loss to you and it might better serve the interests of the Eastern country," he answered, "That may be so, but our giving up of that claim would mean for us a diplomatic defeat. The British are trying to eject us from the East and we will not be ejected." While discussing the Eastern situation with an English scholar and publicist in London, I asked him, "Do you not think the time has come for England to begin withdrawing from India and Egypt?" he answered, "The trouble is if we should leave those countries some other European Power would jump into our place, and would

72

not be likely to do those countries nearly so much good as we are doing them." So there seems to be a sort of divinely appointed mission for every European Power to perform in its particular "sphere of influence" in the East and to keep its alert rivals out of where it thinks it ought to be.

Here we are able to gain some insight into what is known as "the Eastern Question." The original conception of this Question arose from the dealing of the European Powers with Turkey. What to do with the possessions of the "sick Man of Europe" was to those Powers the Eastern Question. But with the widening of the European conquests in Asia, the Eastern Question has become much more inclusive. In its essence this Question is: How can the European Powers divide the Eastern world among themselves without eating one another up in the process? So long as there are two or more rival European Powers in Asia there will be an Eastern Question. Diplomatic triumphs and diplomatic defeats, spheres of influence and markets for the output of European industries, will always provide the fuel for the fierce fire of rivalry. The state of mind of each one of those colonizing Powers is like that of the man who said that he always felt unhappy to think that another man's land bordered on his.

Chapter Sixteen - The Results

WHATEVER may have been the causes which led them thither, the European Powers are now in the East and have been there for many generations. That in course of time they will find it advisable and necessary for them to leave Asia may be taken for granted. When that will be it would be hazardous to prophesy. Perhaps before the present century ends the miracle will have been wrought. And it is good to keep in mind that the European conquests of Asia have not all been cruel: that there was at times a conspiracy of circumstances beyond the will and design of either the East or the West which led a European Power to occupy an Eastern country, and that these conquests have not been planned as means of revenge of Asia's ancient aggressions against Europe.

Let us now ask and try to answer the questions, namely, What effect has this European invasion, political, educational, and commercial, had upon the East? To what extent has it changed the life of that ancient world? Has the change been baneful, or helpful, and conducive to world-peace?

As may be readily assumed, opinions here widely differ. There are those who assert that the East's contact with the West has greatly altered the East's modes of life and thought, and that on the whole the change has been for the better. There are others who maintain that the effect of the West upon the East has been more apparent than real and more harmful than helpful. Such opinions prevail among the observers and appraisers of those changes, in both the East and the West. The larger number of the former group are to be found among the missionaries and those others of merchants and states-men who believe that the East sorely needs the West's tutoring and guidance. The Easterners also who are of this opinion are those who compare the con-ditions of life in the East, before the European influences penetrated it, with those conditions to-day and find that decided improvements have been ef-fected. This favorable opinion, however, was more prevalent in the East be-fore the World War than it has been since. Those who hold the contrary opin-ion in the West are to be found largely among the "liberals" in politics and religion - the haters of imperialism and lovers of all mankind - and among the "nationalists" in Eastern countries. Not a few of this class of thinkers are to be found also among those who, while not opposed to the invasion of the East by the West, hold that, from an economic as well as a political point of view, the enterprise is not a paying one. At least, leaving the past out of con-sideration, the adventure is no longer profitable.

Speaking of the influences of the West upon the East in an earlier chapter, [1] I said, "The Greeks, the Romans, the Crusaders, and the more recent im-perialistic colonizers of Gauls and Saxons have, all of them, sought to awaken the East from its deep slumber and lead it to the fresher springs of their own civilization, but to little purpose...In the process of the centuries that hoary Orient threw off the thin veneer of alien civilizations as a healthy person throws off a cold, and resumed the even tenor of its way." In fact the effects of the East's conquests of the West have been far wider and more lasting in the life of the West than those exerted by the West upon the East.

The dominant races of Europe are nearly all of Asiatic descent, deriving their blood from more or less recent invasion and colonization from the East. ...Europe, in fact, is a great conterminous colony of Asia, which, in the course of thousands of years, has set up for itself...We are indebted, however, for far more than racial descent to our Eastern progenitors of the remote past. Leave their descendants where they are to-day, but withdraw from them the basic discover-ies and inventions which we owe to Asia, and the entire fabric of our existing social arrangements would collapse. Cotton, silk, porcelain, the mariner's com-pass, gun-powder, algebra, geometry and astronomy, as well as much of our ar-chitecture and agriculture, with many of our fruits and flowers, came first into our daily life from that continent. Every one of the great religions of the world, to say nothing of philosophy, was vouchsafed to humanity from east of the Mediter-ranean Sea. Our own Asiatic religion, Christianity, is so overlaid with so much of Greek metaphysic and pagan ceremonial that the unlearned are apt to think of it as a purely European creed. [2]

Of Asia's non-receptivity of Western ideas Mr. Hyndman has this to say:

There is nothing to show, either in arms or in arts, in philosophy or in religion, that the Asiatics, who were compelled to submit for the time being [to Alexan-der's rule] adopted Greek methods or absorbed Greek ideas...The wave of inva-sion receded and matters went on below the surface as they did before.

Even the Roman mastery of a large portion of Asia scarcely influenced Eastern thought and Eastern customs at all. Yet this second great European invasion lasted for many centuries...Those long, long years of peaceful and successful rule failed to impress European conceptions, or European methods, upon the mass of the subject population, or even upon the educated classes as a whole. They remained essentially Asiatics, in all important respects, below the surface...The great legacy of administration, laws, and jurisprudence which Rome bequeathed to Europe proved of little virtue in Asia. [3]

The general opinion of this author is that the changes which modern European invasions will produce in the life of Asia will be not much greater than those of the past.

I wish to quote another and more recent English writer on the effect of the British occupation upon India:

Britain has governed India now for many years; in some parts for two hundred years...During all these years she has directly or through native Princes preserved peace and order throughout the length and breadth of the country eighteen hundred and three thousand square miles of dense population and has carried through the best piece of police work on a large scale which has ever been known in the history of the world...Thirty-seven thousand miles of railway have been made; canals have been constructed to irrigate twenty-seven million acres of what was often desert land; ten universities have been opened and a network of schools has been spread over the country. Western surgery and medical treatment are now within the reach of all who need them. Immense quantities of private capital, mostly British, have been invested in railways, coal mines, tea gardens, cotton mills, jute mills, woollen mills, and recently even in steel factories. Foreign business houses and banks have been established all over the country; they have opened the markets of the world to the produce of India, and have enabled her to buy on credit from the ends of the earth. This is the material prosperity which English rule has brought to India.

But man cannot live by bread alone, nor can a nation's growth be tested by the amount of steel it imports, broadcloth that it consumes, or gold that it hoards. The question which calls for a candid answer is whether India shows any spiritual progress also, during the years of British rule, and, if she shows little or none, why this is...The truth is that little or no spiritual progress has resulted from all our efforts to lead India along the path of Western civilization. The reason is that the spiritual food provided has consisted of strange foreign ideas, and the spirit has become sickly from the unnatural diet and longs for the simpler home fare. It could not be otherwise. To the Hindu the ideal of life is one of contemplation - the Englishman lauds action; the Hindu is imaginative - the Englishman is a rationalist; the Hindu is a fatalist the Englishman thinks himself freer than he is; the Hindu is sublime in his resignation - the Englishman, like Jacob, wrestles even with God.

The unrest is not chiefly political, nor to be cured by a change in the form of government; it was social before it was political, and arose from the constant irritation of exotic ideals at every point of contact with an alien government and society. The great mass of the people even now think, feel, and will just as they did under the Moghuls, Mahrattas, or Sikhs, and it is the policeman's eye, not any change of heart, which has modified conduct. The few who have really come under the influence of Western culture have read, marked, and learned, but have seldom inwardly digested; they have been like actors uneasy in their fancy dresses, and playing parts into the spirit of which they could not enter. They are types of the hybrid failures which longer Western rule would multiply all over the country. [4]

Generally speaking, I think the views of the writers just quoted are sound. I believe a correct understanding of the Eastern mind will justify their hopes and their fears. But our question calls for a consideration of the changes which the Western invasion of Asia has wrought, not only with regard to the extent of those changes, but also with regard to their character. That they have not penetrated the inmost depths of the soul of Asia is, I think, a fact which every correct and fair-minded observer of present conditions in the East must admit. But so far as they have gone, have they been beneficent or not?

It is, of course, very difficult, if not impossible, to trace the influences of such great movements of thought in all their ramifications and be able to make a definite estimate of their values. All such influences, whether exerted by commercial, political, or educational conquests, are in the last analysis spiritual in character, therefore most subtle and elusive. To say that no good at all has come to the East from its contact with the West would be sheer folly. On the other hand, to pretend to know in every case the qualitative changes wrought by this contact would be hazardous in the extreme. My own estimate of Western influences upon the East may not be free from the bias which personal benefits seldom fail to create. For I am strongly inclined to think that, but for my contact with Western educators in Syria, even slight as it was, my lot either in the Old World or the New would not have been as happy as it is. Even Western commercial and industrial enterprises in the East have been beneficial to it in more than a material sense. With these, especially at the hands of the Englishmen, have come a better economic order for the common people within reach of those enterprises, a far more impartial administering of justice, and a doing away with some of the cruelties, such as the burning of widows in India and the flogging of the fellah in Egypt.

The history of the Western religious missions in the East, both Catholic and Protestant, contains many luminous chapters. The Jesuit is a great missionary. Both as a preacher and as an educator he has the faculty of impressing himself mightily upon his human environment. The Protestant missionary, while less intense than the Jesuit, is freer in thought and thus better qualified to keep pace with modern progress. Missionary institutions in the East, especially the educational, have been the chief awakeners of its forward-looking men and women. Such institutions as Robert College and the Constantinople College for Girls in the capital of Turkey, and the American University in Beirut, Syria, have their great cloud of witnesses among the modern thinkers of the Near East. Not so much can be said for the purely religious work of Protestants in that part of the world. But for the educational institutions that work would in all probability have been given up long ago. The reason of this is not that the missionaries have not been zealous in their preaching, but that the East does not need to be "converted." And it should be said in the interest of truth and justice that the first Protestant missionaries in the East were not convert-seekers. Their initial purpose was to be teachers within the existing churches of the ancient communions and carry on a work of religious education. This they were allowed to do, especially within the Greek Orthodox Church, until their work began to bear fruit. Their liberalizing influence, such as it was, soon aroused the apprehensions of the bishops and induced them to anathematize the followers of the Protestant teachers. Then it became necessary to provide a spiritual home for those followers who were disowned by their Mother Church. But the Protestant converts have been comparatively very few, and their small churches almost wholly under missionary control.

But the story does not end here. The deeper reason for the non-receptive attitude of the East toward a Western presentation of Christianity is to be found in the earlier history of the whole Christian movement. The fact that Christianity never had the hold on the East which Mohammedanism later acquired was due to the profound changes which speculative Western theologians affected in the simple message of the New Testament. In the early centuries of Christian history the message of the Gospel, so strangely changed in the West, was brought back to the East as an exotic plant.

The Christian Church had its simple origin with a group of Jewish followers of Jesus Christ in Palestine, but it had its marvelous expansion and organization among the Gentiles. In Palestine the faith of the Church was very simple. Faith in God the Father, and in His Son (by anointing) Jesus Christ, and love of the brethren, constituted the simple creed of the Palestinian Christians. But it was not long after the Crucifixion when the subtle mentality of the Greek and the organizing genius of the Roman began to assume control of the thought and practice of the Syrian churches. Simple faith in Christ was forced to be hospitable to intricate scholastic statements of doctrine, and "love of the brethren" gave way, as a bond of union, to ecclesiastical authority. In course of time that simple faith was supplanted by the massive creeds with all their metaphysical speculations about the nature of God, the status of Jesus in the cosmos, and the mystical character of rites and sacraments. Such metaphysical profundities, which had little or no bearing on life, made but a slight appeal to the Oriental mind. A Westernized Christianity could command the allegiance of only a small number in the native land of the simple Jesus, and was almost swallowed up altogether by Islam.

Thus the modern Western missionary in the East finds himself at a great disadvantage. Whether he preaches the creed which he has inherited from the ancient church councils, or the simpler gospel of the good life, he tells an old and familiar story. To the ecclesiastical Christians, as to the free and vital Mohammedan communion, this new preacher appears to be quite unnecessary. As an educator, however, the missionary is no small factor in the new intellectual awakening which is beginning to purify both Christianity and Mohammedanism of their crudities and errors.

For various reasons the beneficial effects of Western activities in Asia have not gone deep into its life. To the people in general the foreign agencies remain foreign and are becoming even disagreeably so (as will be seen in the next chapter) with the passing of time. Neither the foreigners nor the natives have been able during these many years to bridge the racial and social chasm which yawns between them. The real connecting links are as yet very few. The Westerner does not mean to be Easternized and the Easterner does not seem able to become Westernized. The glowing accounts of some writers, largely "observing" travelers and over-enthusiastic missionaries, of the changes which have taken place among the intelligent classes of the East would induce the belief that every Easterner who speaks a European language and wears a European costume has been thoroughly Europeanized. The facts, however, do not sustain such a view. Yet the misconception is not at all strange. The formal social intercourse between Europeans and educated Orientals seldom fails to convey such an impression. The Westerneducated Oriental knows enough of the etiquette of such occasions to enable him to meet the European with ease as a social kin. The test, however, is not thorough enough here to bring out the real facts. Those racial and social aliens meet under Eastern skies, but they do not *live together* long enough to know how radically they differ from one another with regard to their respective modes of life and thought. The only sure way of knowing what the members of a certain race are is not simply to study their behavior toward foreigners whom they meet only occasionally, but their behavior toward one another in everyday life.

My own recollections of the attitude of educated Syrians toward their Western educators and others in their midst may shed light on this point. So far as I can remember, our attitude toward the foreign missionaries was on the whole respectful and grateful. We thought of them as men and women who had come into our country to preach and to teach in obedience to Jesus' command, and of their activities, so far as they went, as beneficial to our people. There were some among us who thought that those missionaries were the disguised political agents of their home governments, but this idea never was extensively prevalent, nor, in fact, disagreeable to us, seeing that we had no great love for our Turkish rulers. But, so far as I know, and barring out the few exceptions on either side, we never felt that we were deeply in love with those foreigners nor they in love with us. They had their ways and we had ours. We criticized them (sometimes uncharitably) in the privacy of our gatherings, and we thought they did the same to us among themselves. Friendships between the two elements were not rare, and racial enmities did not exist to any appreciable extent. But there was no real amalgamation in any sense. We lived after our Syrian fashion, excepting that some among us wore the European costume with the Turkish fez, and they lived after their European and American fashion, and none of them wore the native Syrian costume. Their homes and institutions and all their premises were, according to the extraterritorial guaranties, foreign territories, and they could be tried for any offense only at their respective consulates, or in the Turkish courts by consent of their diplomatic representatives and in their presence. So far as I know these same conditions are substantially the same to-day in the East as they were at the time I have spoken of. Social intercourse between the educated Orientals and their Occidental visitors is as a rule cordial and refined. A cultivated Oriental family is one of the finest beneficences of civilization. Occidentals of true spiritual culture recognize this and esteem it as the surest sign of promise for the future of the Orient. However, whether we consider such families, which are as yet comparatively few, or the mass of the people in relation to the Occidental in their midst, the East and the West remain two separate entities.

The Western-educated Easterner in Europe and America differs in some important respects from his educated kinsman who lives in the East. In Europe and America the environment is such that it constantly works for the dominance of the Western over the Eastern mind in this individual's life. In the East the case is just the reverse. There Western culture is an imported plant constantly subjected to the powerful action of Eastern influences. Not having sprung from the life of the people themselves, it can have but a slight effect on them. If such educated persons should in some unaccountable way become thoroughly Westernized, they would be detached from the human lump which they are supposed to leaven.

It may be desirable to convert the East into the ways of the West, but so far success here seems to be impossible. The East has derived many benefits from the West, although not so many as those which this younger world derived from the East in earlier centuries. Let us hope that for the good of civilization in general this interchange of benefits may continue, with improved methods of transmission on both sides. Now we come to the question: If the effects of the modern Western invasions of -the East have been on the whole beneficial to it, why then is it in a state of revolt against its beneficent invaders? I shall try to answer this question in the following chapter.

[1] Opening paragraph, Part I, Chapter II, ante, page 23.
[2] H. M. Hyndman, *The Awakening of Asia*, pages 1, 2. (Boni and Liveright, New York.)
[3] *The Awakening of Asia*, pages 3-4.
[4] From an article entitled, "India's Revolt Against Christian Civilization," by W. S. Hamilton, I.C.S., retired, in *The Hibbert Journal*, April, 1922.

Chapter Seventeen - The Revolt of the East against Western Domination

THE title of this chapter describes a fact which can no longer be reasonably denied. Whether we consider Japan with her armed determination to keep herself free from foreign interference; or half-awakened China, yawning, stretching, and rubbing her eyes on her way to full national consciousness; or India using her ancient mystical weapon of non-resistance in boycotting her invaders; or the Moslem world driven to active resistance by the memories of a great past and the sense of present humiliation under foreign rulers; or any other Asiatic people - we find the East in a state of revolt of varying intensity against Western domination. The revolt is not only in the air; it is in an actual state of condensation and precipitation.

The complex cause of this state of things involves mysterious and indefinable elements. "The spirit of the times" is one of those baffling forces which compasses a people's paths and stimulates it to action in a way incomprehensible even to the wisest of its leaders. National boundaries are far from being spirit-tight barriers between peoples; and there seems to be such a thing as a common atmosphere which all peoples breathe. The pressure of new influences may lead peoples to imitate and love one another, or to grow more zealous for their own modes of life and thought and become mutually antagonistic. Again, alien invaders, as the Europeans in the East, whatever their actual purposes, obviously never fail to arouse in the minds of the invaded apprehensions and fears whose extent and intensity go beyond the regulations of rational thinking. Under such circumstances incidents which seem in themselves trifling, irritations and antipathies which appear light and transient in character, as well as weightier matters, all converge in that super-consciousness we call a people's soul and cause it to act as by a power beyond and above itself.

The East to-day is in such a state. It is moved to revolt against its alien invaders by a power higher than all its conscious designs. The movement is more than racial, more than religious. It is a sectional uprising; the East as a whole is facing the West. The Asiatic peoples, divided as they are among themselves, are drifting into a unity against the Europeans. The Chinese, the Japanese, the Hindus, the Persians, and the Arabs; the yellow, the brown, and the white races of Asia are confederating in spite of themselves. The ancient continent seems to be emerging into the consciousness that it has a soul of its own which must not be allowed to be destroyed. Such a sense of unity may not be of an enduring character, but is at present very evident. It is a defensive force born of the present necessity.

So far as can be seen, the Asiatics are not at present thirsting for blood. They heartily prefer to rid themselves of their Western masters in a peaceful and friendly way and to open their markets and institutions, as free peoples, to the Western traders and educators. But good faith between the West and the East is being destroyed by the imperialistic diplomats and merchants on the one hand, and the fiery fanatics on the other. If this state of things should continue much longer, it would not be at all strange if Asia and Europe should find themselves in the not very far future in battle array against each other. The spirit of hatred is spreading in the East with the consciousness of humiliation which the attitude of Europe is deepening in the Eastern peoples.

While in Paris during the Peace Conference, a friend of mine, a French-educated Syrian, related to me the following incident. While calling on an accredited Oriental diplomat in that city their conversation turned on Eastern affairs. The diplomat in question was neither of my friend's faith, nor race. But seeing that his Syrian visitor was of Oriental birth, the diplomat opened his heart to him in startling fashion. Pointing in the direction of the place where the Peace Conference was meeting, the Oriental dignitary said, "Young man, we can expect no justice from these Western nations. They look down upon us; they *despise* us. All we can do now is to await our day; to wait until they are weakened by their luxuries and vices, as they are being weakened, and dissipated by their wars and then set upon them and crush them."

As yet this is not the spirit of the Oriental peoples in general, but it is the spirit of many of their leaders and is finding its way into the ranks. Such spirit must not be allowed to control the actions of the peoples of the East. The Western nations can easily check it, not by might nor by power, but by genuine acts of justice and good will toward the East.

I have said that the East is now driven into rebellion against Western domination by a mysterious power higher than the East's conscious designs. Yes, but it is also conscious of more concrete causes which it is now stating to the whole world. It feels that the general attitude of the West toward it is one of contemptuous superiority. This feeling would seem highly exaggerated when one thinks of that class of Westerners whose thoughts toward the East are thoughts of peace and good will and who are to be found in every country in Europe and America, but not when one thinks of the Western world at large, especially its governments.

At least for the last three hundred years, during which period the power of the sword has been transferred from the East to the West, the Occident has cast its awesome shadow over the Orient. It has looked upon the Orient, especially that part of it known as the Near East, as upon a social and political world whose course in history has long ago reached its terminus; a world whose faith, genius, racial and national spirit, and its recuperative powers have only a name that they live, but are dead. To the Western merchant the East has been simply a market in which he could trade on his own terms. To the Western diplomat that ancient world has been a practically defenseless region in which, with only a little display of force, a "sphere of influence" could be established. His theory is that the Oriental may cry and grumble and curse in the face of aggression, but if dealt with in a "firm manner" he soon yields and submits to the inevitable. He is by nature a fatalist and is prone to accept whatever is imposed upon him as his divinely ordained *kismet*. His history proves conclusively that "he is not fit for self -government," therefore it becomes the philanthropic duty of the Western Powers not to give the Easterner enough rope to hang himself, but to rule him for his own good.

The Western missionary, while sharing the views of his kinsmen, the merchant and the diplomat, concerning the helplessness of the Oriental, comes to his aid with more beneficent intents. The twofold imperative urged upon the missionary, first to obey his Master's command, "Go, ye, into all the world, and preach the Gospel to every creature," and, second, to save the perishing soul of his Oriental brother, provides him with a far more exalted motive than either that of the merchant or the diplomat. As a spiritual diagnostician, however, the function of the missionary (especially of the old type) has been to look for sin, and not for virtue; for defects, and not for perfections. So, in describing the Easterner to the benevolent people of the West, the missionary, apparently with no intention to misrepresent, emphasizes the ills to which our mortal being is heir. So, whatever the intents and purposes of those Western commercial, political, and religious imperialists may actually be, their resultant activities make the East appear to the West as a helpless dependent utterly incapable of regaining its self-reliance. The Oriental, however, in spite of all the tutoring his invaders have bestowed upon him, is not yet fully convinced of that. While he realizes that, compared with his Babylonian, Hittite, Aramaean, Phoenician, and Arab forefathers, he is now in a retrograde state, nevertheless he still feels that he has a soul which holds immense possibilities and is capable, not only of regaining its heritage, but of establishing a future even worthier than the past. He realizes also that if he only had powerful fleets and armies to defend his realms his civilization would be perfectly satisfactory to his Western contemporaries. In any case he doubts, and for good reasons, their philanthropic intentions toward him. He considers them hostile invaders.

The awakening which certain classes of Easterners have experienced as a result of Western activities is also contributing materially to this spirit of unrest. The greatest opponents of the foreigners are to be found among their own pupils. This is neither strange nor should be ascribed to ingratitude; it is the legitimate result of the new education. The enlightened Easterner says to his Western teacher, "You have taught me to seek the truth fearlessly; you have instilled in me the idea of nationalism; you have spoken to me passionately of freedom and democracy; you have clearly pointed out to me the fact that in your country men are equal and the citizen is a sovereign individual; you have taught me both by precept and example that men must die if need be in defense of their individual and national rights; you have awakened me to the fact that national education only can produce national heroes, that the fruits of commerce and invention must be conserved as national assets; and called to my attention many other things for which I thank you. I find, however, that when I try to put your precepts into practice and seek to be free and to build up a free nation with free institutions, you check me with an iron hand. You call me a rebel against your authority in my own home. In your country a revolutionist against injustice and foreign rule is enshrined as a great hero and patriot, but the revolutionist in my country against you as a foreign ruler you call an adventurer and a fanatic. In your country you consider education in a foreign language to be disloyalty to the flag, but you make your language the medium of education in my country. You come to change my manner of life, but if I should go into your country on a similar mission, you would cast me out as a 'degraded Oriental.' Therefore let me say to you, 'Rend your heart, and not your garments'; let me have the substance, and not only the form of your education; I am willing to have you as my teacher and adviser in the things that I need to have and learn from you, but if I am to be the man your education calls for, I must be free from your domination and your air of superiority."

One of the very recent and most striking illustrations of this state of mind is to be found in the anti-French attitude in Syria. As will be stated more fully in a later chapter, the large majority of the people of Syria are strongly opposed to the occupation of it by the French. This is not altogether strange; but what seems rather amazing to the French themselves is that their severest critics, one might say their worst enemies, among the Syrians are graduates of French schools - the very men from whom France had expected the most loyal support in the carrying-out of her Eastern policy. And what is proving rather an embarrassment to the French in this controversy is that their Syrian opponents do not take as a basis for their argument abstract theories of government, but the very principles upon which the French home Government itself rests. Many of those Syrians have studied, not only in French colleges in the East, but also in Paris. They are well versed in French history, especially that part of it which records France's heroic struggles for freedom and democracy. They ask their French rulers whether "Liberty, Equality, Fraternity," is a good motto for France, but a bad one for Syria. They ask that if France is "the mother of liberty" in Europe, how comes it that French armies are sent forth to conquer and subjugate other peoples? Why is it that, while the Syrian agitators in France itself against the French occupation of Syria enjoy the privileges of free men, in Syria such agitators are seized by the French authorities and thrown into prison?

A free and democratic nation engaged in an imperialistic enterprise anywhere in the world finds it most difficult to give honest and satisfactory answers to such questions.

Again the Eastern peoples find that the foreign enterprises in their midst, of whatever description, are not of their own choosing. They have been forced upon them by the will of peoples more powerful than themselves, not always actually, but virtually, by the sword. The superior Powers of Europe mean to give the Eastern peoples what they think those peoples should have, whether of schools, commercial establishments or forms of government, regardless of their consent or refusal. Behind those beneficences are not thoughts of peace and good will, but fleets and armies. No sooner does a foreigner establish himself in an Eastern country than he becomes master of the house, and the native virtually an alien. The dictum of Western statesmen is that the European in the East "must either rule, or go." This is true. Eastern methods of government do not fit the mentality of the European nor fully accommodate his modes of living. But the awakened Easterner is now asking whether he has a right in this age of the world to rule himself in his own way. What would the European do if the tables were turned and the Easterner come to rule *him* in his own country? Would he be likely to accept the situation as a foreordained and inevitable thing?

But the plea of many Western thinkers is that the Oriental is not fit to rule himself. This was said of Japan seventy-five years ago, and is now said of China and other Eastern countries. It is generally true in the sense that the Oriental method of government is not like the Occidental method. The East-erners do not wish to promise to govern themselves in such a way as to suit the Occidental's views of government in every particular. They would adopt Western methods in so far as the necessities of their own life require. They would establish reciprocal relations with Western Governments, as well as among themselves; but they want first of all to be permitted to live their own life in their own way. They realize that in the last analysis what the European nations are so deeply concerned about in this regard is, not so much the sta-bility of government for the East's own sake, but for the protection of the investments of their own nationals in that part of the world. This the East-erners do not mean to disregard. At least for their own interest they would welcome and protect such investments, but they would be governed here by their own laws, as other peoples are. The great European nations are doing business with other nations, such as the Balkan States and some South Amer-ican countries, whose governments are not so stable as those of the great nations themselves. They have in those countries educational institutions, missionaries, and great commercial and industrial enterprises, yet they do not demand, because of these enterprises, to exercise authority over those small nations. Their reciprocal relations with them are maintained through diplomatic agencies and the laws which govern the conduct of nations to-ward one another. Why not deal as generously with the Asiatic countries? Would not India be as safe to trust in such matters as Mexico, and Syria as Ecuador?

Among the great agencies also which are spreading the spirit of revolt in Asia are the works of Western writers, both friends and foes, which deal with the problems of the East. Such writers portray for the Eastern peoples their exoteric and esoteric states of existence as only very few, if any, of their own leaders ever could do. Western historians trace the great events which have shaped the life of the East with such clearness and accuracy as to reveal the Oriental to himself in a manner which urges his heart to vaster issues. Through such studies China emerges out of the mist of the centuries with her poised mind whose creative power anticipated the West in many inventions which this youthful world thinks it has originated, and with a marvelous system of ethics which is still fit to guide the life of a twentieth-century civilization. Mystic India comes forth with the dreams of countless generations preserved for her and for the world in shrines and temples and a literature whose spiritual depth no plummet has yet fully sounded. Her philosophy streams forth deep and rich with the spiritual contemplation of long ages and shames the utilitarian precepts of this feverish and restless age. Persia is called forth to tell the stories of her great poets, kings, statesmen, and artisans. Syria is called to remembrance as the giver to the Western world of nothing less than its saving faith and deathless scriptures. Small, yet great; poor, yet making many rich; dying, yet she lives in the life of every civilization worth the name. The Moslem world is revealed as an organic whole whose life-center is a simple faith in the one God - a faith strong and vital, whose banners have never been carried by cowardly men. The conquests of Islam, spiritual and intellectual, have left behind them an awakening glow of glory which even enemy nations feel compelled to admire, and a Community of Believers who, despite all their faults, have always loved one another more than the Christian nations have ever loved one another. There is no need to speak of the history of Japan. This once "hermit nation" is now in the front rank with the great nations of the West as a living example of the copious vitality and rich possibilities of the soul of that ancient East. Japan stands as a warning to the despoilers of Asia. Both through her might and her peaceful counsel she says to Western imperialists, "The sword of conquest cuts both ways; other Asiatic peoples are on their way to where I am; if you are bent on sowing the wind in Asia, then prepare to reap the whirlwind."

In this way Western writers are revealing the East to itself. They are interpreting to the Eastern peoples their life in a manner which tends to awaken their pride and make their discontent with the European's methods in dealing with them ever more dynamic. What the Easterners achieved in the past is urged upon them as a bugle call to future deeds - to freedom from foreign domination, to faith in themselves and to a deeper response to the appeals of modern progress.

Nor is this all. The Western interpreters of the history and life of the East are providing the Easterners with the technique of revolution. Consciously and unconsciously they are telling those peoples what they themselves would do, if they were in their place. The Hindus are told what to do to make England's position in their country untenable. The "non-cooperative movement" in India is not wholly Oriental in origin. You will find the suggestion in Western publications antedating Gandhi. The Moslem world has been told a hundred times what it might do to rid itself of its alien rulers if it once regained its collective consciousness and unfurled the banner of the prophet to the breeze. The Syrians are being told to-day in various ways by liberal French politicians what to do to render impotent French designs in Syria and compel the withdrawal of the French forces from it. Any Eastern country to-day rising against its European master could easily secure arms and munitions, if not military tutors, from some other European country, with sincere wishes for complete success. The West is arming the East both mentally and materially, and, if saner counsels do not take the place of the madness of imperialists the conflict cannot be very long deferred.

Yet, notwithstanding all this, if the promises which were made by the Allies to the Eastern peoples during the World War had been faithfully kept, the accumulated wrath of former years would not have reasserted itself with such increasing intensity after the decisions of the Paris Peace Conference were made. Nearly all the East was on the side of the Allies in the great conflict. The Eastern peoples contributed men and money with lavish hand. Their men fought bravely, and hosts of them laid down their lives as martyrs in the cause of freedom. To them, as the Allies told them, the war was a war of liberation, not only for Serbia, Belgium, and France, but for them also. The glittering promises of the Allies seemed to those Orientals pure gold. They trusted their leaders as children would their parents. To them the dreams of years were to be fulfilled in the great victory. The day of liberation was as sure to follow that triumph as the evening the morning. And when victory was achieved, the hopeful, anxious Orientals flocked to Paris as to a Pentecostal Jerusalem.

Chapter Eighteen - The East at the Paris Peace Conference

WHAT the world expected from the Paris Peace Conference is still too fresh a memory to need extended mention. Excepting the few seasoned statesmen whose plans finally prevailed, the untold millions of the suffering nations looked upon the Armistice as the terminus of a sad old world, and upon the Peace Conference as the beginning of a new and beatific order. At that clearinghouse of an exhausted civilization the Book of Judgment was to be opened and the secrets of all hearts revealed. All duplicity, treachery, greed, hatred, and every other trait of the "old diplomacy," were to be cast out into the outer darkness, and a new humanity, chastened by suffering cleansed and tranquillized by repentance, and baptized with the Holy Ghost and with fire, established in the earth.

It was not only the Fourteen Points which like a bright star of hope led the representatives of the small nationalities to the capital of France. The repeated declarations of the Allies during the war, that the mighty struggle was being carried on by them for the liberation of all oppressed peoples, and the fascinating effusions of war-time orators concerning "the ideals we are fighting for," also acted very powerfully to convert the timid hopes of the oppressed peoples into certainties. The war-time promises gave the fundamental principles of the new world order, and the Fourteen Points the method by which those principles were to be applied.

It was both touching and amusing to observe the state of mind and the conduct of those pleaders for the oppressed during the early stages of the Peace Conference. They seemed like children on Christmas Eve. They were all more or less acquainted with the promises of the Allies and the Fourteen Points. Their implicit faith in finally winning the right to "self-determination" seemed a foregleam of the millennium.

But notwithstanding the solemn character of those expectations the situation had a decidedly comical aspect. Every representative of a racial group in Paris had a map defining the region which he thought was his people's legitimate inheritance. In every case the delimitations were so clear that a wayfaring man though a fool could not possibly fail to appreciate their fairness and correctness. That the border lines so marked often cut into areas occupied at the time by another people did not much matter. The owner of the map had his carefully studied argument justifying the inclusion of the new territory. His ancestors once lived in what is now another people's home, and simple justice required that the stolen territory should be restored to their descendants. He could by appealing to archaeology prove that the ancient fragments of architecture found in the coveted region were of the exact type his own people used, and by appealing to philology demonstrate that traces of his mother tongue were still to be found in the language of the neighboring community. His people, he would assert, had been waiting these many years for the day of "self-determination," and now that day had come. To him the case was so simple and the claim so obviously just that only the most willful disregard of the right on the part of the peace negotiators could prevent the success of his mission. The right must prevail! The men who were supposed to have influence with the Powers that be were besieged by these earnest pleaders for the small nationalities. At hotels, on the street corners, as well as at their offices, the "specialists" attached to the various commissions, many of whom had no influence whatever with their chiefs, were relentlessly implored to intercede with their superiors for a long-oppressed people. The arguments of the various pleaders were so similar in form and substance that those who were fated to listen to them had a standardized answer which they gave to almost every one of the would-be liberators of the oppressed nations.

The Eastern peoples great and small were represented at the Paris Conference. Japan, China, India, Persia, Arabia, Syria, and Armenia were there. But the only Eastern nation which received respectful consideration from the Great Powers was the one which was well armed. Japan rode on a tide of power and secured what she asked for. When her representatives threatened to leave the Peace Conference if they were not granted their demands, especially with regard to Shantung, the great statesmen acceded to those demands with as dignified cheerfulness as was possible under the circumstances. But when the representatives of China tried to play the same game, if their territory was taken from them and given to Japan, no one seemed very seriously to care. The statesmen "could not satisfy every one." India was, of course, a part of the British Empire, therefore could not negotiate independently. Armenia was given much sympathy while she was being abandoned to the wolves. The chief representative of that long-tortured country, Boghos Nubar Pasha, was an able statesman, highly cultured, and a most gracious gentleman. Very few of the representatives of the small nations had the access to the principal peace negotiators which he had. Dignified, eloquent, resourceful, earnest, firm, he never failed to make a deep impression upon his hearers whenever he had the opportunity to plead for his poor country. But all was in vain. No careful observer of events at the great Conference could fail to see that Armenia had been deserted from the time it was left, according to the terms of the Armistice, as Turkish territory whose fate was to be determined "later." At the end of three months of ceaseless endeavor on his part to save Armenia, I met Nubar Pasha at the British headquarters. "My dear sir," I asked the grand old man, "what is the latest news?" "I am glad to see you," he said to me. "Misery loves company. What do you think the latest news is? They have just told me that Armenia *is still Turkish territory*, because the Allies did not occupy it during the war."

The fact was that Armenia seemed to the imperialists very uninviting. Economically it is not a paying proposition. Diplomatically its position between the Turks and the Bolshevists is highly undesirable. It does not, like Syria, form a connecting link between three continents, nor is it the historic home of three great religions. Armenia might deserve a few tears as a much-afflicted country, but it does not pay as a "sphere of influence." Why, therefore, not leave it as a means for future settlement with the Turks, or, as the best humanitarian measure possible, offer it, with all its problems, to President Wilson? This the cautious statesman gladly did. Mr. Wilson would have accepted the trust so humanely offered to him, but for good or evil the American people or their representatives were not so ready to concur in the matter. Armenia has since been handed back to the Turks, with the promise of European "protection."

The case of Syria and the Arabic-speaking world in general was different; and because of its bearing on future events in the Moslem world it deserves extended consideration.

In order to have a clear comprehension of the cause of the present unrest in the Arab world, especially in Syria and Mesopotamia, it is necessary to give a summary of the war-time negotiations between the British and the Arabs, and the British and the French. It is a well-known fact that the two European Powers which exercise the widest control in the East are England and France. While these two great nations were contending with the Central Powers on the field of battle, they were also contending against each other diplomatically with regard to their future status in the Arab world which bordered on the Mediterranean. France, realizing the strategic position of Syria as the highway between the Orient and the Occident, and falling back upon her ancient claim to being the protector of the Christians of the Near East, demanded the whole of Syria as her sphere of influence. To this England objected. She demanded that part of Syria known as Palestine as a sphere of influence for herself, which, she maintained, was necessary for the safety of the Suez Canal and the security of her highway to India, and that the province of Damascus be put under a native Arab ruler. However, the claims of the Arabs, who were ready to turn against their Turkish rulers if the Allies were willing to grant their demands, conflicted radically with the French and English claims. The pressing necessities of the war, however, led the British to enter for the time being into negotiations with the Arabs, and, again, with the French, which apparently were never intended to be faithfully adhered to. And here I prefer to have a British writer [1] give an account of those negotiations.

It was said this writer at a very early stage of the hostilities that special efforts were initiated to detach the Arab population from their suzerains, the Turks, and, largely through the instrumentality of Lord Kitchener, who knew Palestine and Syria as no other living Englishman, negotiations were opened with his friend, Shareef Husein [2] of Mecca. In a letter to the High Commissioner in Egypt in July, 1915, the Shareef asked, before taking up arms for the Allies, "that England should acknowledge the independence of the Arab countries bounded on the north by Adana and Mersina up to the 37th degree of latitude, on the east by the frontier of Persia up to the Persian Gulf, on the south by the Indian Ocean with the exception of Aden, and on the west by the Red Sea and the Mediterranean up to Mersina."

Replying in October, 1915, the High Commissioner wrote: "I am empowered in the name of the Government of Great Britain to give the following assurances: Great Britain is prepared to recognize and support the independence of the Arabs within the territories included in the limits and boundaries proposed by the Shareef."

To cut a long story short, the passive resistance of the civil population in Palestine and the active cooperation of the Arab forces on the right flank of the British as the fruit of these assurances, were two of the most important factors in Lord Allenby's great victory. The Arab forces were led by the sons of the Shareef, one of whom, the Emir Feisal, now king of Irak, escaped from Turkish captivity to join the Allies.

This undertaking with the Arabs involved also negotiations with the French, who had always, since the days of Saint Louis, laid claim to special interest in Syria...A conference was held in London in October, 1915, at which the French were represented by M. Georges Picot; but nothing was accomplished at this meeting since the French claims embraced the whole of Syria and Palestine, and there was no ground for discussion. Later, however, in 1916, an engagement was concluded, known from the names of its negotiators as the "Sykes-Picot Agreement," by which Syria was divided into three spheres of influence, the British having Palestine, the French the rest of Syria, except the province of Damascus, which was left to native rule.

In these negotiations we have a fine specimen of the old diplomacy. As may be readily seen, Syria was included in the Arab countries the independence of which Shareef Husein had asked England to recognize as the condition on which the Arabs would enter the war on the side of the Allies. This demand was granted, as Lord Kitchener's official communication to the Shareef clearly shows. Not long after this, England entered into an agreement with France, as above quoted, according to which Syria was practically taken out from among "the Arab countries" and divided between these two Powers into spheres of influence. And, to make confusion worse confounded, another perfidious document was issued later in the war. In order to allay the suspicions of the Arabs, which had begun to manifest themselves at a most critical time in the war, and to assure the Washington Government that their intentions toward the Eastern countries were those of disinterested liberators, the British and the French issued jointly, in the latter part of 1918, the following declaration:

Text of declaration agreed to between the British and French Governments and communicated to the President of the United States of America.

The aim which France and Great Britain have in view in waging in the East the war let loose on the world by German ambition, is to ensure the complete and final emancipation of all those peoples so long oppressed by the Turks, and to establish national governments and administrations which shall derive their authority from the initiative and free will of the peoples themselves.

To realize this, France and Great Britain are in agreement to encourage and assist the establishment of native governments in Syria and Mesopotamia, now liberated by the Allies, as also in those territories for whose liberation they are striving and to recognize those governments immediately they are effectively established.

Far from wishing to impose on the peoples of these regions this or that institution, they have no other care than to assure, by their support and practical aid the normal workings of such governments and administrations as the peoples shall themselves have adopted; to guarantee impartial and even justice for all, to facilitate the economic development of the country by arousing and encouraging local initiative, to foster the spread of education, to put an end to those factions too long exploited by Turkish policy - such is the part which the two allied governments have set themselves to play in liberated territories.

There can be no doubt that President Wilson's address at Mount Vernon, July 4, 1918, was the major cause of the above declaration. In that address Mr. Wilson said:

The settlement of every question, whether of territory, of sovereignty, of economic arrangements, or of political relationship upon the basis of the free acceptance of that settlement by the people immediately concerned, and not upon the basis of the material interest or advantage of any other nation or people which may desire a different settlement for the sake of its exterior influence or mastery.

Of course this statement was taken by the Syrians and the Arab countries in general to mean that Mr. Wilson and the Allies were in perfect accord with regard to the settlement of political affairs in the Near East. In other words, by Mr. Wilson's utterances the Eastern peoples were induced to renew their confidence in British-French promises. This and the subsequent declaration quoted above appeared to those peoples to nullify any other agreement those Powers might have had between them with regard to the Near East. The very clear declaration by them that their purpose was "to establish national governments and administrations which *shall derive their authority from the initiative and free will of the peoples themselves,*" added to President Wilson's far more sincere utterance, brought the representatives of the Arab countries to Paris with heads erect and hearts glowing with hope. They were led to believe that finally the Christian nations had decided to give the Golden Rule a fair trial. The Peace table was to be a communion table at which the bread and wine of human brotherhood was to be partaken of by the heralds of a new and nobler age.

The decrees of the great Conference dashed all such hopes. It seemed to those Easterners to uncover the moral nakedness of Europe. Instead of dissipating, it greatly intensified, the hostile feeling which they had had in previous years toward the Europeans. And what was sadder still was the fact that while before that great conclave of diplomats, the Easterner's dislike of the European nations was mixed with respect; after it, that dislike became deeply saturated with contempt. At Paris the Eastern countries found no redeemer. They had been pawned in advance by diplomatic gamesters and had no voice whatever in the determination of their destinies. England thought that her control of Mesopotamia and Palestine (where, in direct violation of her agreement with Shareef Husein and her later pledge to respect the wishes of the native population, she had generously invited the Zionists to establish a "national home") was necessary to the safety of the British Empire; France had "sentiments" about Syria, which could not be properly ignored; Italy felt it her solemn duty to mother Asia Minor; and even Greece thought her ancient traditions, as well as her present interests, required that she should be the stepmother of some section of the East. It was, however, *pure philanthropy* on the part of those nations which led them to rival one another in seeking spheres of influence in the East!

Notwithstanding my experiences at the Peace Conference, I still have faith in human nature. I even still hope that some day the East and the West will come to a fraternal and mutually beneficial understanding, even though I cannot dispel the belief that the Conference has greatly weakened the probability of such consummation.

The treatment at the Peace Conference of the pleaders for the small Eastern countries was of the comi-tragic sort. Prince Feisal, son of the King of Arabia, came to Paris to represent his father and to plead for self-government for Syria. To the French, however, he was England's guest. I was sent to Paris as the representative of Syrian societies in this country. The plan of our societies was, if Feisal's sincere purpose was to secure for Syria true national existence, to join forces with him in pleading for the unity and future independence of that country. If the Near East was to be placed under the mandatory system, our plea was to be for an American mandate, or none. In any case we did not want a French mandate for Syria. Prince Feisal received me as a friend and we almost lived together all during my stay of three months in Paris. He declared himself in perfect harmony with our plans, and being at the time the military Governor of Syria he was, of course, the chief negotiator for it. We soon learned, however, that the unhappy country we had come to plead for had already been divided and "attached" by England and France. But Feisal, persuaded in his own mind that, as the lineal descendant of the prophet of Arabia, he was in Paris as the symbolic image of fourteen centuries of Mohammedan history, felt perfectly confident that he was able to alter any previous agreements with regard to Syria between those great nations. "The past is past," said the confiding Feisal to me when I first met him. "Now, brother, we are in the hands of friends and we shall secure our rights." The outcome of the negotiations, however, rudely dashed this hope.

The Kitchener Agreement with Shareef Husein was for the most part forgotten, the joint declaration of England and France was ignored, and the Sykes-Picot Treaty made the basis of negotiations.

The idea of a mandatory system for the Eastern countries was first definitely put forth in the League of Nations Covenant as presented to the Peace Conference, February 14, 1919, as follows:

Certain communities formerly belonging to the Turkish Empire have reached a stage of development where their existence as independent nations can be provisionally recognized, subject to the rendering of administrative advice and assistance by a Mandatory Power until such time as they are able to stand alone. *The wishes of these communities must be a principal consideration in the selection of the Mandatory Power.* [3]

Feisal and the rest of us were glad to accept this plan, provided the wishes of the Arab countries were given "a principal consideration in the selection of the Mandatory Power." We all realized that those countries would at the beginning, and perhaps for a period of years, need the friendly assistance of a Western Power in steering the course of their political destiny.

As is well known, owing to the fact that the United States was not technically at war with Turkey, President Wilson could not enter into the settlement of Turkish affairs as a principal negotiator, except as they were brought before the whole Conference. However, in pursuance of his own ideas stated above and with reference to the Franco-British declaration of 1918, he made the excellent suggestion that before the fate of Syria was decided an international commission should be sent to that country to ascertain if possible what Mandatory Power the people there would like to have. The representatives and other friends of Syria hailed this suggestion as the best means possible to solve a very knotty problem. The English also appeared most agreeable to it; the French, however, looked upon it with grave suspicion. "Why is it," was their question, "that that part of the East where we assert it is our right to go should be so treated?" M. Clemenceau said with grim humor, "Why not send such a commission to Egypt and India and Mesopotamia to ascertain what Power those countries want to mother them?"

Nevertheless, for the moment the French agreed to the proposition. England, America, and Italy were to be the other participants. The English made out that they were highly delighted with the plan. President Wilson at once appointed Mr. Charles R. Crane and Dr. Henry C. King, President of Oberlin College, to head the American group. For a brief period of time all seemed very harmonious. Feisal was jubilant. He knew and I knew that America would be our people's first choice, with England as a possible second, in case America refused to accept the trust. The French Government knew that also; consequently they promised to join in the commission and cancelled their promise, if I remember right - and I cannot forget - seven times in nine weeks. The representative of the French Foreign Office who was empowered to discuss the problem of Syria with her representatives told me one day: "You may be sure we shall never consent to the sending of this commission. And if we should be persuaded to join in it, we never should accept its recommendations. We know that such a report would be adverse to our interests. The British [army of occupation] have been in Syria for several months intriguing against us; they have poisoned the minds of the Syrians and made them anti-French."

"But why," I asked that dignitary, "does the French Government deem it its duty to occupy Syria, while fully ninety per cent of its people do not want you there?"

"We have strong sentiments about Syria," he replied. "Our schools and our missionaries have been there for generations. Besides," he added, with an altruistic air, "if we should leave those people alone they would cut one another's throats."

"Why don't you let them do it?" I spoke again. "What have you been doing for the last four years in Europe but cutting throats on the most colossal scale the world has known? The Eastern peoples ruled themselves for centuries before France was born and still they have more throats than they can feed."

"Our views on the subject," he answered, "are different, and we have the power to carry them out."

But the remark of Prince Feisal when I reported the conversation to him is worthy to be perpetuated. It expressed with great conciseness the mind of intelligent present-day Orientals. "Can you tell me," he said to me, with a disdainful smile, "why our throats are so dear to these Western imperialists?"

The attitude which under the circumstances Prince Feisal acquired toward European diplomacy affords another interesting specimen of Oriental psychology. Notwithstanding the prevailing Western opinion that the Easterner is constitutionally unveracious, his fundamental instinct is faith. He trusts where he cannot see. He *believes* and has spoken it to the world that the way of the kingdom of heaven is childlike trust. His passive and contemplative mind is keyed to confidence. His far-famed trickery ends with small things. "Weightier matters" awaken both his integrity and his faith. So Feisal, whose knowledge of the rich and various resources of European diplomacy was rather limited, implicitly trusted his Western guides. With this simple trustfulness he came to Paris to gather reinforcements from friendly camps for the reawakened national aspirations of his people. The rod and the staff of this trustfulness failed him. The time and environment were not right for it. Suspicion with him soon gained on confidence. He was soon forced to fall back on the one instinct of self-preservation.

The son of the Prophet became gradually averse to any sort of mandatory control. The vacillating attitude of France toward the proposed commission angered and emboldened him. He began to talk of "calling Syria to arms." "You know," he said to me one day, "what will happen in the East if I but say the word." Alarmed at this because of what I realized such an uprising would mean to the scattered Christian communities in the interior of Syria, I turned to him, clasped his hand, and said, "I trust Your Highness never will find it necessary to say that word. Such a course would certainly be disastrous for Syria."

The final stage of those negotiations began with a remark which Mr. Lloyd George made to Feisal at a reception at President Wilson's residence. Shortly before that the Prince had told me that the French Government had notified him "officially" of their consent to have the international commission proceed to Syria, and that he had decided to leave Paris within a few days in order to be in Syria when the commission arrived. At Mrs. Wilson's reception I was standing with Feisal when the very cordial British Prime Minister approached, shook hands with the Prince and indulged in a few pleasantries. Of course "shop" talking was not the most suitable thing for the occasion, but Feisal's traditions were different from those of an Englishman. He at once asked Mr. George whether he was certain "the commission was going." The great Welshman replied with a smile: "It all will depend on what sort of agreement you will make with Mr. Clemenceau. If you two can agree on a plan the commission will not need to go. [4] You had better see Clemenceau. He is a fine old man and means to do what is right." That alarmed the Prince; it meant to him that after all the commission was still in suspense. M. Clemenceau also came and greeted Feisal with a handshake, but no conversation followed. On our way back to Feisal's residence, he said to me, "I shall see Clemenceau, but if we fail to agree, I shall proceed to Syria, raise and equip an army, then let them [meaning the French] come and take my country away from me."

The momentous interview with the Tiger, as the Prince told me, "was pleasant," but apparently not of a decisive character. The French terms were very liberal. In fact France was willing to grant almost any terms, provided she was allowed to come into Syria, officially recognized as the Mandatory Power. Feisal was afraid to accede to any official French claims whatever. He objected to having the French flag over Syrian soil. He was promised that that flag would be raised "only over French army headquarters in Syria." He replied that Syria was a quiet and a friendly country and needed no French army. The native troops were amply able to maintain order. His final demand was that France should recognize the complete independence of Syria, then in return he would promise "as a gentleman" to turn to France first for any assistance Syria might need to further its development and progress. Apparently Feisal came away from that meeting convinced that Clemenceau had conceded his demands.

It was late in the evening three days later when Feisal sent a messenger asking me to come at once to his residence. He had just received a diplomatic communication from the Quai d'Orsay signed by the Premier. It was intended to be a written confirmation of that "friendly conversation." It may have been due to a failure of memory on the part of the Prince, but he declared to me with fiery emphasis, as he handed me the precious document, that its contents were essentially different from the "conversation." He felt that he was being tricked to agree to stipulations injurious to his cause. Turning to me, and with a gesture which seemed to sweep over all Paris, he said: "Is this what you call 'Christian civilization'? Do those who are known as great men tell lies so easily?"

"No, Your Highness," I replied; "I do not call this exactly Christian civilization, and I beg Your Highness to realize that this kind of thing is not lying; it is diplomacy!"

The general tone of the French document was most friendly. Its terms were also liberal.

The French Government [it said] acknowledges to Syria the right to independence as a federation of locally autonomous provinces in accordance with the traditions and desires of the population...owing to the needs of the country, the interests of the population, and the ancient role played by France...France is the Power qualified to render Syria assistance and provide her with various necessary counsellors to establish order and bring about the progress which the Syrian people demand. When the time comes for the elaboration of the detailed arrangement to assure the collaboration of France with Syria, it should be in conformity with the spirit of our conversation.

Of course the "spirit" of a conversation is in such matters a very elusive thing. The acknowledgment by France also of Syria's "right" to independence was rather indefinite. And why the Prince should agree at the very beginning to having France provide Syria "with necessary counsellors to establish order" was not clear to him. His conversation with the two representatives of the French Government who carried the official paper to him on that evening was anything but friendly. After their departure, the Prince, some of his staff, and I had a long discussion of the situation. He was ready for war against France. I remarked that such a war without England's help would be disastrous to our cause, and that it was not conceivable that England would render Syria such a help against France who was her friend and ally. He replied, "At any rate the lion fights to the death in defense of his lair." His final decision on that evening was to have another interview with Lloyd George the next day; if more favorable terms could then be obtained, well, but if not he would proceed at once to Syria, put his army around him, and dare the French to come and drive him out.

The meeting with Mr. Lloyd George, at which I was present, was very significant in that it definitely revealed to Feisal the attitude of the British Government toward the Syrian question. The remarks of the Prime Minister were clearcut and apparently very sincere. In a very cordial manner he gave the Prince to understand that he and M. Clemenceau were to solve the Syrian problem among themselves. Feisal remonstrated.

"Clemenceau wishes to occupy Syria," he said in heated accents. "Do not let us fall into the hands of the French; if they go into Syria they will want to Frenchify us and that will mean our annihilation. We want independence."

"But," said Lloyd George, "the Council of Four has decreed that the small Eastern countries must be mandated; that is final."

"Then give us an Anglo-Saxon Mandatory Power," said Feisal; "we do not want France."

"But," replied Mr. George, "we have a treaty with France with regard to Syria, and France demands the enforcement of the terms of that treaty. It is a bad treaty, I admit, but we have signed it and we cannot go back on our signature. The fact is," he added, "we cannot go to war with France over this matter. In the first place, France is our friend and neighbor; in the second place, such a conflict would destroy what is left of civilization."

"If you do not fight France, I will," said Feisal, with an uplifted hand.

"That," said the Prime Minister, "would be most unfortunate. I hope you will see Mr. Clemenceau and discuss this matter again with him in a straightforward manner. He is a business-like man and wants to do what is right."

At the conclusion of the interview Feisal left in bad temper. I suggested on our way home that as a last resort he should accept the most liberal terms France could offer him, accept her mandate and leave the question of complete independence to the future. This he would not do. He would go to Syria and carry out his plans of "defense." He did go to Syria and there set in motion forces which later he could not control. He returned from there to London. The French continued to offer him liberal terms, but he would have nothing short of complete independence. He returned to Syria and was crowned King in the city of Damascus. His first act was a decree ordering "all foreign Powers" to withdraw from Syria, as the country was able to take care of itself. The French forces, however (as will be more fully stated in the next chapter), under General Gouraud attacked and dethroned Feisal. He fled to

England, thence went to Irak, where, in the summer of 1921, he was, with the consent of Great Britain, crowned King of that country, where he now rules.

[1] Vivian Gabriel, in an article entitled "The Troubles of the Holy Land," the *Edinburgh Review,* January, 1922.
[2] Shareef Husein is now King Husein of Hedjaz.
[3] Italics are mine.
[4] The international commission was finally given up. President Wilson, however, sent the American Commission alone. The report of this commission has never been published by the Washington Government. The supposed reason of this is that, as the people of Syria were, according to this report, overwhelmingly in favor of America and against France as a Mandatory Power for their country; and as America did not wish to accept the trust herself, the Washington Government has suppressed the report in order not to jive additional cause to the Syrian Nationalists to resist the French, nor to France to believe that America is not in favor of the French policy in Syria. But the substance of this report has been published by Mr. Ray Stanard Baker in the *New York Times* of August 20, 1922, and it fully supports the views I have already stated concerning the aversion of the Syrians to a French mandate.

Chapter Nineteen - The French in Syria

THE army of occupation in Syria after General Allenby's defeat of the Turks was overwhelmingly British. Only a small number of French and Italian troops participated in the Syrian campaign - just enough to make the happy conclusion a victory of the Allies, and not of the English only. France was at the time engaged in fighting the great battles of the war at the Western front, therefore could not very well spare many troops to send to Syria. As soon, however, as the two Powers proceeded to carry out the terms of the Sykes-Picot Treaty, the British troops began to withdraw from Syria (except Palestine) and French troops to take their places. It was this movement which, as was stated in the previous chapter, Prince Feisal had gone to Syria to resist.

It will be remembered that according to that treaty the province of Damascus was to be under native rule, with an Arab prince as its executive head. This stipulation, as I learned from reliable sources in Paris, was not at all agreeable either to the French or to Feisal. "Do not think for a moment," I was told by a prominent Frenchman, "that if we go to Syria we are going to be content with that western edge, The Lebanon, which cannot produce enough to feed itself. The interior also must be under our control and we must have the oil wells of Mosul. When we go to Syria we intend to rule." This attitude of mind on the part of French statesmen was conditioned by the suspicion that the British were trying to outwit them. The latter's position with the Arabs was and is far stronger than that of the French. King Husein owes his throne to the English. The French could see that the Arab prince who was to rule Damascus very likely would be one of King Husein's sons, most probably Feisal; therefore he would be a tool of the British. With such a ruler in Damascus, with the British in Mesopotamia and Palestine, with another Arab prince in the East of the Jordan province, and with the Turks in Asia Minor, the French position in the rest of Syria would be anything but desirable. How could they hope "to rule" with any security while beset with so many foes? The plan of the French, therefore, was either to take Feisal under their wing, as it were, or, failing in this, to drive him out of the country by force.

Feisal, on the other hand, was no more anxious to abide by the letter of the Sykes-Picot Treaty than the French were. In the first place, what right had the British and the French to make such a treaty and div r de an Arab country between them? In the second place, how could the province of Damascus live and prosper and expand her commerce and industry without an outlet to the sea? The French held the coast-line and thus placed Damascus at their mercy. Feisal's plan, therefore, was to rid himself of France altogether, and in course of time, if fortune favored, drive the British also out of the neighboring provinces. His father's agreement with Lord Kitchener guaranteed the *independence* of the Arab countries, and that great consummation was his goal.

The vast majority of the people of Syria were anti-French. But a very significant minority - the Maronites of The Lebanon, not a few of other Christians, and some of the Mohammedans - was, much more then than now, pro-French. There was also many of that "certain element" with which every country is afflicted, the seekers after the loaves and the fishes, who are always "pro" the ruling power, whether it be an angel or a devil, Saxon, Frank, or Turk, who when they found that France was to hold a protectorate over Syria began to shout *"Vive la France!"* But Syria is a Moslem country. Of its three million inhabitants about two and a half millions are Moslems. It is for this reason that the Christians, who are largely in The Lebanon and of the Catholic faith, have always sought the protection of a Christian Power, especially France. They have always contended that a native government in Syria is bound to be a Moslem government inspired by the ancient enmity which has always existed between the Christians and the Mohammedans. And taking into consideration the Moslem population as a whole, this suspicion can by no means be considered groundless.

The leading Mohammedans of Syria, however, stoutly maintain that a native Syrian government would be of the people and for the people, regardless of sect or creed. Many among them even interpret the Koran in such a way as to show that this supreme and final authority is not at all opposed to a form of free government under which all sects may enjoy the privileges and the responsibilities alike. This state of mind was revealed to me by Prince Feisal in Paris with evident sincerity. As an Eastern Christian who knew something of the old order and as a representative for the time being of a section of Syrian opinion, I deemed it my duty to put the question to the Prince in the simplest and clearest manner possible.

"Your Highness," I said to him, "what aspirations do you personally have with regard to the future government of Syria? Do you intend to claim it as part of your heritage as the son of the King of the Arabs and descendant of the Prophet? Furthermore, do you think that after Syria has been set free the Mohammedans who are the majority of its inhabitants would be likely to assert their claim to be its rulers and put the Christians under tribute as in the past?"

Looking me squarely in the face and reenforcing his words with artless but effective gestures, the Prince said: "Brother, Allah witnesses between us that I have no personal ambition. My deepest desire and the goal of my endeavors are to see not only Syria, but every Arabic-speaking country, free and self - ruled. I want the people to choose their own rulers and every ruler to be bound by a constitutional law of the people's own making, in order that no personal ambition can find occasion to assert itself." Then, with a sudden flash in his gentle eyes, he exclaimed, "By the Almighty, if my own brother should seek to destroy the freedom of the Syrian people, I would be the first one to fasten the noose around his neck!"

After an impressive pause of a few seconds, the Prince said: "As to your second question, I will say that it would be rash for me to pretend to know what every individual Moslem thinks. However, so far as I know, the Mohammedans of Syria are desirous of doing away with religious distinctions and differences as regards governmental matters. The past is a warning to them. If they should be enticed in the future to emphasize their religious differences, they would lose their freedom, and most deservedly. I believe that I speak for the vast majority of Moslems when I say that our ardent desire is for a free native government in Syria in which men of all sects and no sect shall take part."

This seems to be the attitude of a large number of Syrian Mohammedans. Some of the educated Christians consider it to be honest and sincere, while many others take an opposite view. They assert that such promises were made by the Moslems when the Turkish Constitution was first promulgated, but they were not kept. The Moslems have yet to give tangible evidence of their good intentions to live with their Christian neighbors on terms of perfect equality, without being compelled to do so by a European Power.

At this point, however, let me say that it was this state of fear among the Christians which gave France the occasion to proclaim herself their protector, and to demand the right to exercise control over the whole of Syria as the only way in which she could maintain peace.

"You know what will happen in the East if I but say the word," said Feisal to me in Paris. It would seem that upon his return from Paris, angrily disappointed at the failure of France unqualifiedly to recognize the independence of Syria, the Prince did say that "word." [1] Serious disturbances began to occur in various localities, especially along the borders of The Lebanon, which the then small French garrisons could not always quell. Naturally the Moslems did not attack their own people. Christian villages and towns were pillaged; murder, rape, and other atrocities were committed against the Christians, because they were thought to sympathize with the French. It seemed for a time that anarchy would soon sweep the whole country.

In one sense those disturbances tended to serve France's purpose. They tended to substantiate her claim that if she did not exercise firm control over Syria the Christians there would be destroyed. In the early days of the "occupation," however, the French troops came into Syria in small numbers. The French apparently did not wish to convey the impression that they had come as invaders. But as the disturbances increased, military wisdom required quick action before the situation got completely out of hand. The task was committed to no less a military genius than General Gouraud, and French troops began to pour into Syria in great numbers. The hour of decision as to who was to rule Syria, Feisal or the French, was at hand.

It was in March, 1920, that the "National" Assembly in Damascus proclaimed Feisal King of Syria, and a native government was established. It was, of course, intended to be a strictly constitutional government patterned somewhat after the English system. The Government was in the hands of the Cabinet which was responsible directly to the National Assembly or Parliament. As I have already stated in the preceding chapter, King Feisal's first great act was to issue a decree proclaiming Syria an independent and united country and ordering the military forces of foreign nations to leave it, as "the country was able to govern itself." Notwithstanding this, however, the disturbances continued to agitate the country and the suffering communities to cry to both the Damascus Government and to the French for help. Meantime, while perfecting his military preparations, Gouraud continued his efforts to conciliate Feisal and lead him to accept the French terms. The state of the country required that the French forces and the Feisal Government should act together, and such cooperation could be secured only by Feisal's recognition of France as the Mandatory Power for the whole of Syria. Gouraud's efforts bore no fruit. To the Damascus Government, the French in Syria were invaders who should be expelled.

In July, 1920, the French general found himself compelled to move against the Turks who were still carrying on military operations in the direction of Aintab. His troops had to pass through territory which was under the Arab flag. Feisal, although the Turks were his enemies also, refused to permit the French troops to pass through his domain. Thereupon, on July 15, 1920, Gouraud sent an ultimatum to King Feisal giving him forty-eight hours in which to decide between accepting the French terms or fighting. Feisal decided to yield, but the Nationalists checked his course. The forces which he had set in motion had gone beyond his control. He stood between two fires. He was suspected of being insincere by both the French and his own people. The Nationalists were "ready for war" in defense of home and altar, regardless of the King's wishes. The reply to Gouraud's ultimatum failed to arrive at the appointed time. It was stated afterwards that Feisal did send a reply "on time" accepting the French terms; that the telegraph operator at Damascus did "tick" the momentous message, and that it failed to reach its destination because, as was later discovered, "the wire had been cut." Who cut the wire, the French or the Nationalists? The mystery has never been cleared. Another version since published by some anti-French Arabic newspaper was to the effect that Feisal's message failed to reach Gouraud because, on the day it was due, the French telegraph operator at Riak, a point halfway between Damascus and Beirut, was instructed not to transmit to the commanding general any messages from the Damascus Government. How they came by such information has not been stated.

But what really alarmed the French and compelled them to act was the fact (according to French reports) that during the "forty-eight hours," as the French airmen observed, large bodies of Arab troops were entrenching themselves at Maiselon, a strategic point about twelve miles west of Damascus. Upon hearing the report, Gouraud ordered his general in the field to attack at once. For the first hour the Arabs fought with great courage and effectiveness. The good news caused the civilians to stream out of Damascus, armed with every imaginable weapon, "to help the army crush the invaders." But soon the tide of battle turned. The terrible French artillery and air forces poured streams of fire upon the gallant Arabs. In three hours and forty minutes the Nationalist forces were completely shattered. The civilians who had come to fight remained to implore the French to receive the surrender of ancient Damascus without firing upon it. The French accepted. Gouraud levied a penalty of ten million francs upon the city, sentenced many of the Nationalist leaders to death, and warned the population that, if they killed a single French soldier or any of the Christians, their city would be destroyed. Feisal fled to the south, harassed not so much by the French as by his own people. Some laid the responsibility of the fatal engagement upon him, while others accused him of willfully neglecting adequately to prepare for the defense of the country.

Ever since the "Day of Maiselon," the French have been the masters of Syria. So far their task as the pacifiers and protectors of that country has been neither easy nor agreeable. The spirit of revolt against them seems to grow stronger as time passes. The complex cause of this can be learned only through an impartial survey of the controlling circumstances.

The French entered Syria under most adverse conditions. Could they, through some quarrel with the Sultan, have gone into that country fifteen or twenty years ago, they would have been welcomed as deliverers. They would at least have occupied a position similar to that of England in Egypt, and have finally evacuated Syria, if the circumstances required, in a manner which in all probability would, even without a treaty, have given France the position of the "favored nation" with the Syrian people. Twenty years ago the Syrians were anti-Turks, and not anti-French. The Arabs then had not been as they were during the war promised independence and then had it denied to them.

The French would not have come into Syria "authorized by the Allies" to exercise dominion over it, but by one of those "accidents of history" to which the East had been long accustomed. As it was, the French invaded Syria at the end of a war which threw almost the whole world into confusion. The entire East was aflame with wise or misguided aspirations. The Eastern peoples had lost their reverential regard for the European Powers and were in a state of defiance. The French and the British not only failed to unite in a cooperative policy in their dealing with the Arabs, on the one hand, and the Turks, on the other, but entered into a diplomatic war with each other. The French also were very much afraid, as was intimated to me in Paris, that if America should be induced to occupy Syria and Armenia, the result would be, not only "too much Anglo-Saxonism" in western Asia, but also the elimination of France from that part of the world forever.

France, therefore, dreading a diplomatic defeat, insisted on her "right" to occupy Syria, according to the terms of the Sykes-Picot Treaty. Upon her arrival in Syria, France found the Lebanonians ready to receive her, but not with the unanimity and warm cordiality she had expected. The rest of Syria she had to fight into submission. To-day in front of her stands her uncompromising enemy, Feisal, and his Irak kingdom ready to fight her. On her left flank in the East of the Jordan province is his brother, Abdu-Allah; on her right flank are the Turkish Nationalists in Asia Minor, who are in constant communication with the anti-French elements in Syria; and south of her are her rivals, the British, in Palestine.

As was to be expected, the French found Syria in a deplorable condition as a result of the war. Desolation, hunger, disease, fear, discontent, rebellion, loss of faith in the powers in heaven above and on the earth beneath, were all there. The French were expected by their Syrian friends (and their enemies would have been much reconciled 'if those expectations could have been met) to put Syria again on her feet and give her even greater than pre-war prosperity, with magical swiftness. Of course this would have been impossible to accomplish even by a country like America with her unlimited resources which the war barely touched. How much more difficult, therefore, it must be for France in her exhausted condition! With Syria restless as it is, even the mere cost to France of the large army of occupation is proving a burden grievous to bear. Furthermore, when the French began the work of rehabilitation in Syria the enormously high cost of labor and material compelled them to levy such taxes as drove the war-impoverished people into rebellion. They began to cry for the Turks, who did not make so many "improvements" nor, consequently, levy such unheard-of taxes. [2] The Nationalists claim also that the freedom which they had expected to enjoy under the French has proved to be a mirage. The press of the country, they vehemently assert, is, as regards political matters, subjected to the strictest supervision, and that the suppression of newspapers which venture to discuss politics is quite frequent. The French language, they also maintain, threatens to supplant the Arabic language and the people are in danger of being in course of time "Frenchified."

Taking all these things into consideration, it is, I think, not difficult to see what task the French in Syria have on their hands, the worst feature of which is their inability to win the confidence of the people. And it is substantially true that the best and ablest French statesmen are averse to accepting positions in their country's colonial administrations; therefore such positions, which require a different sort of wisdom, are largely assigned to military men. Such is the state of things in Syria to-day. French rule is military rule. It is conceivable that the French are already weary of their task in Syria, but how could they leave it without suffering that dreaded "diplomatic defeat"? What bearing would their withdrawal from Syria have on their North African colonies? Even the contemplated withdrawal of the British from Egypt and the likelihood of their following a similar course in Mesopotamia is making the French position in those colonies, as well as in Syria, very insecure.

What England, for an example, might have done in such circumstances cannot, of course, be safely conjectured. What seems to be a fact, however, is that the policy of the French in Syria has been so far a policy of suppression. Their reaction to the adverse conditions betrays fear and nervousness. The logical French mind has no "shock absorber." The law of cause and effect acts upon it mercilessly. For an example, the British are the diplomatic rivals or enemies of the French in the East; therefore it follows that every English-speaking visitor, or even dweller, in Syria is most likely a British spy. It must be presumed that he is "guilty" until he is proved innocent. Again, the majority of the Syrian people do not look with favor upon the French occupation; therefore any popular demonstration by those Syrians must be considered an incipient revolution.

Last April, Mr. Charles R. Crane visited Syria. Mr. Crane seems to have deep interest in the East; Asia has great fascination for him, especially the Moslem world. His having been one of the principal members of the American Commission sent to Syria by President Wilson made the people of Damascus flock to him on this recent occasion and present to him their grievances. It is very probable that the majority of the Damascenes did not know that Mr. Crane's present visit to their city and country had no official significance whatever; that he was traveling only as a private citizen. His statement to the press was that he said nothing whatever during his stay in Damascus that could in any way have misled the people to believe that he was on a political mission, or an agitator against the French. The people, however, held a great and noisy demonstration in favor of "independence," and begged Mr. Crane to present their cause to the great American Nation. They were unarmed and peaceable throughout. But to the French the incident seemed fraught with grave danger. They at once applied force; they fired upon the crowd, seized the leaders, tried and sentenced the "guilty" ones for from ten to twenty years' imprisonment. Mr. Crane was suspected of having gone to Syria for the purpose of fomenting revolution, but he finally succeeded in clearing himself of the charge.

Military rule is never conducive to harmonious relations between a people and their rulers, especially when the rulers are aliens. The soldier knows how to fight, but as a rule he is unfit to exercise the functions of a statesman or to administer justice.

Let us now turn to Syria itself and its internal problems. The Syrians are justly classed with the civilized peoples. So far as their natural endowments are concerned, they possess the proper credentials for admittance into the company of civilized thinkers anywhere in the world. They are by nature neither cruel nor lawless, are very responsive to kindness, and have deep reverence for moral and spiritual ideals. The Syrian is intellectually strong and is certainly a poet and a spiritual genius; but like the majority of Easterners he is not an able administrator. He is not so strong as a public man as he is as an individual, and the tyranny of centuries to which he has been subjected has prevented him from remedying this serious defect. He is unable to see things in the large, and to subordinate partial interests and racial allegiances to national interests and the common welfare of the whole people.

But Syria's gravest problem is the religious disharmony which exists between its various sects. When a religious prejudice is thought to have divine sanction, it becomes irremovable. It has not been altogether a blessing to the world that the devotees of each of the three great religions of the world - Judaism, Christianity, and Mohammedanism - have always considered their own religion to be the only true one which must put all other religions in subjection to itself, if not extinguish them altogether. Judaism, however, has for centuries ceased to be an Eastern problem, and Christianity would have followed the same course but for the support given to it by the European nations. Mohammedanism, as I have already stated, is the dominant religion in Syria, and it remains strongly militant. To its adherents it is "the true faith" which must tolerate no rival. This does not mean that the Moslems have always been cruelly intolerant of the Christians. No; their history shows that they have been invariably well disposed toward an inactive, non-militant Christianity in their midst. They have been more generous toward Christians completely under their control than the Christian sects in the Middle Ages were, or now are in certain parts of Christendom, toward one another and toward the Jews. And I very much regret to say that the Christian sects in Syria have by no means been a shining example of brotherly love toward one another; and it is rather doubtful whether, if they and the Mohammedans exchanged places, they would be more tolerant toward the people of the Koran than these have been toward them.

But if Syria is to attain nationhood and take its place among the civilized nations of the world, her people must build for the future on other and firmer foundations than their religious prejudices. They must endeavor to keep the unity, not of forms and creeds, but of the spirit in the bond of peace. Here the greater responsibility rests upon the Mohammedans. They are the controlling power in the land. Their great literature is its literature and their traditions and laws are at the very foundation of its social life. Because of the fascination of that literature for us, we Christians of Syria and all the Arabic-speaking countries, although of various origins, have always loved to call ourselves Arabs. The Mohammedan of the better type (and I speak of the traditional enemy of my people) possesses many noble qualities. He is brave, dignified, hospitable, true to his faith and ever ready to die for it, a lover of poetry and literature, a spiritual thinker, and a true and loyal friend. The Mohammedan Arab, as a type, is not cruel by nature, but he is somewhat antiquated, and his loyalty to the letter of his religion militates against his true progress. His literature, noble as it is in many ways, is surcharged with the spirit of conquest. It depicts for him in a most thrilling manner the victories of his fathers over the "infidels," and tends forever to urge him to similar deeds. No other chapter in history is so full of glorious deeds of conquest as that which records the events of the first hundred years of the history of Islam. Now the Mohammedan of today is both enriched and handicapped by such memories. He is right in making the thought of such an heroic past the means by which to resist foreign invaders, but he is wrong in thinking that all of what was thought good and serviceable in the remote past may be safely applied in its totality to the present.

The driving of the French out of Syria would not necessarily mean for it a united and happy existence. Negations are not constructive forces. Syria's first and supreme need, with or without the French, is a true national spirit which shall hold in its embrace all her forward-looking men, regardless of sect or creed. The development of such a spirit is a task whose severity tries men's souls. Double-faced sectarian special pleaders are not fit for it. Mere orators and impatient fiery agitators of unstable qualities cannot accomplish it. Such a task requires men who, without compromising their religious convictions, are able to clasp hands with their fellow-citizens across the barrier of creed: men who are capable of sustained endeavor, able to convert words into constructive deeds, who can think in terms of generations, instead of days and months, and are great enough to subordinate self-interest and sect-interest to the building up of the nation's life. Sectarian warfare and true nationalism can never coexist. Such a warfare tends forever to arrest the development of national leaders and to make cunning and craftiness supersede honest thinking.

So long as the leaders among the Mohammedans and the Christians of Syria feel disposed to deceive one another, believing that by so doing they are serving the interests of their respective creeds, Syria will remain a prey to foreign invaders. It will always be a territory, and never a nation. Its masses, poisoned by the duplicity of their sectarian leaders, never will be able to grasp the significance of the idea of patriotism.

Were the Christians in Syria only an *insignificant* minority, the problem would be very simple. But they are not, either as regards numbers or influence. The educated men among them, taking into consideration the country as a whole, are out of all proportion to their numbers. Their claim to a home in Syria antedates that of their Moslem neighbors. They are industrious, and consequently materially comfortable. They are, especially the Lebanonians of them, no mean fighters. I believe that, even if they were deserted by Europe, they would fight to the death before they would be enslaved again by their ancient conquerors. Let us hope, however, that such a necessity may never arise, but that the Mohammedans and Christians, forgetting the past, may join forces with true sincerity in the effort to place their country in the rank of the freest and most progressive nations. The Mohammedans should realize that, whether France gets out of Syria or not, the Christian nations never will allow the Syrian Christians to be reduced to slavery or exterminated. As Prince Feisal told me in Paris, if the Mohammedans of to-day intend to keep alive the religious hatred of the past they would deservedly lose their freedom. The best way for them to rid themselves of European interference is to deal with their Christian neighbors on terms of equality with themselves.

Having so briefly described the French position in Syria and the country's internal problems, I wish now to devote a few paragraphs to the one problem - the French occupation - which confronts both the French and the Syrians. My own position has, I think, been made clear with regard to the relations of the European nations and the Asiatics. I think the West has no right, either moral or legal, to rule the East. If the Eastern peoples are not as yet fully equipped to rule themselves according to modern methods; if they would suffer if left alone to work out their own salvation, I maintain that they, are entitled to that discipline which suffering only can give. The European nations have had to pass through such fiery trials before they arrived where they now are, without the interference of alien nations.

However, we cannot ignore the fact that a *sudden* withdrawal of the Western nations from the East would inflict upon it much unnecessary suffering. Such vast and numerous agencies cannot be torn off suddenly from a people's life without causing it serious injuries. What is needed is an honest purpose on the part of the European Powers to *prepare* to leave those peoples who are in rebellion against Western domination, in the shortest time possible, consistent with those peoples' safety. The time has passed when Asia was considered an easy and defenseless prey to European adventurers. The conscience of the times revolts against such a spirit.

Will the French continue to say to the Syrians, "We are here to stay"? If so, then let them understand that they are sitting on a volcano. What if they are in Syria by the mandate of the European Powers? Does this necessarily mean any more than that one highway robber is backing up another? What the Syrians need is disinterested helpers, and not exploiting colonizers. They are not much concerned about saving a European nation from "diplomatic defeat" or about enabling her to secure "the oil wells of Mosul" at their own cost. France has yet to prove to them that she is in their midst solely for the good of Syria. If she can prove this, then the Syrians can do no better in the present circumstances than to accept for a time her cooperation in the furthering of their country's progress. Let them first unite as a people and gradually demand in a firm and dignified manner the surrender to them of the positions of responsibility until finally such positions are efficiently filled by Syrians, making superfluous all foreign supervision. France, if this is her real purpose, can render Syria inestimable services. She can develop a system of national education in the language of the country; she can teach the people to think of themselves as Syrian citizens, and not simply as Mohammedans and Christians; she can foster industrial and commercial enterprises and render arable the waste places in that ancient land. France has the opportunity to leave for herself in Syria a debt of gratitude to all generations.

But if France is in Syria, as seems evident, for the purpose of furthering her own interests on the pretense that she is there to protect the Christians, then history will record an entirely different story.

The Syrians strongly suspect, and not without sound reasons, that France's consent to and even encouragement of the division of Syria into small principalities is designed to strangle the ideal of nationalism in the country and weaken her resistance to French domination. They further suspect that the shifting of France's diplomatic fortunes in the Near East may lead her to cede to the Turks such portions of Syria as the growing power of the armies of the Crescent may make necessary to win Turkey's "friendship" for France. The fact that Syria is a mandated territory will not preclude such a transaction. As the Earl of Balfour recently said, "The League of Nations is without power to enforce its mandates." On the other hand the Turks have again drawn the sword with might and are hewing down their invaders. France has already deserted Cilicia to the Turkish Nationalists.

Therefore, if France cannot and will not secure for Syria a free national government, it would be far better for her and for Syria if she would secure guarantees (if she can play that game again) for the protection of the Christians, as she did under the old Turkish regime, furl her tri-color and leave the Syrians to establish a government of their own choosing.

[1] It has since been given out from Paris that, when Feisal was requested to come to that city and explain to the Supreme Council why Syria was in such turmoil, he assured the French that if they left him alone he would quiet the country. To the question of General Gouraud whether Feisal was certain that he could, he is said to have replied, "Yes, because the disturbances were begun by my orders."

[2] The secret of discontent here is "high taxes and no improvements."

Chapter Twenty - The Restoration of the Turks to Power

THE more recent developments in Turkey cannot be very well under-stood without a retrospective glance. A brief account of the attempts' to es-tablish in that Empire a constitutional government according to modern standards will materially assist us to grasp the significance of the later events which led Turkey to join the Central Powers in the World War, and those which later shaped the course of the peace negotiations with the Turks.

The first real attempt to restrict the power and authority of the Sultan by constitutional measures was the one which ended the reign of Sultan Abdul-Aziz, who sat on the throne of Turkey from 1861 to 1876. The uprising was not a people's revolution. It was begun and engineered almost wholly by some of the Sultan's own advisers and generals.

Abdul-Aziz visited the principal capitals of Europe in order to obtain first-hand knowledge of its progressive civilization. Upon his return he seemed strongly inclined to introduce into his country what was termed "Christian civilization." But Abdul-Aziz was not a strong man, He loved the spectacular and was an irresponsible spendthrift. By his extravagance he depleted the treasury of the Empire and by his shallow enthusiasm for things European "made the Palace a center of intrigue for the accredited diplomats of the Christian Powers."

The autocrat was dethroned in 1876, and his nephew Murad proclaimed Sultan. Very shortly after that Abdul-Aziz committed suicide. The news of the tragedy shocked Constantinople to its very center and threw the "conspira-tors" into consternation. They summoned as many as fifteen physicians and surgeons to examine the body of the dead Sultan. Their unanimous verdict was that the dethroned ruler must have taken his own life. His former sup-porters, however, insisted that he was murdered by those who dethroned him, and this notion that "the wicked hands of traitors were laid upon the Caliph of the holy prophet" rooted itself in the public mind.

It soon appeared that Murad was insane. He was, therefore, removed from the throne and his brother, the notorious Abdul-Hamid, put in his place. The wily young Sultan granted his people a constitution and "in all good faith" pledged himself to support the new political instrument. Abdul-Hamid's good faith did not endure long. In less than a year he managed to rid himself of both the Constitution and its originators, the very men who had placed him upon the throne. He charged them with the murder of his uncle, had those of them who did not succeed in fleeing to foreign countries "tried," convicted, and banished to various places in the Empire, where they were assassinated, as seemed evident, by the Sultan's own agents. The great Midhat Pasha, who was the brain of the "revolution," was exiled to Arabia, where, after he had been confined for some time, he was strangled by one of his attendants.

The story of Abdul-Hamid as a ruler is well known to the world. From early childhood until I was twenty-one I lived in Syria as his subject, and I well remember how we had to pretend to "revere" him only next to Almighty God. "Our very lives were a grant from His Gracious Majesty!"

In the year 1908 occurred the "Revolution of the Young Turks" against Abdul-Hamid. This also was not a people's, but an army's, uprising. The old Constitution was demanded by the revolutionists. Finding himself deprived of the support of the majority of his generals and soldiers, Abdul-Hamid "gladly" granted the petition of his "people," declaring that his only reason for abrogating the Constitution thirty-two years before was the fact that the people of the Empire "were not then ready for it." However, in the course of less than a year he again attempted the overthrow of the Constitution. This time, however, the army was still watching the movements of the perfidious Sultan with deep anxiety. The chief body of the revolutionary troops was then at Salonika. From that center those picked warriors marched upon Constantinople, overpowered the defenders of Abdul-Hamid, dethroned him, and placed his brother, Mohammed V, on the throne.

"The final triumph" of the Revolution was acclaimed with shouts of joy all over the Empire. The peoples under the Turkish flag of all races and creeds hailed the Constitution as the holy book of a new and happy era. The Moslem and the Christian embraced one another in the streets as brothers. We former subjects of the Sultan in the New World also joined our kinsmen across the seas (not without misgivings) in their rejoicing and high expectations. We hoped that the rising aspirations for representative government in all the nations of the world would sustain the efforts of the Young Turks and guarantee them success; that the great European Powers would lend the constitutional forces in Turkey all possible aid and thus assure the triumph of an enlightened scheme of government in that Eastern Empire. We loved to think of an Oriental civilization rising in that part of the world and drawing into itself constructive Occidental elements without losing its own desirable features. It seemed to us also that the success of the Young Turks movement would go far toward giving a happy solution to those vexing problems which had long been spoken of collectively as the "Eastern Question."

Needless to say that those hopes failed of fulfillment. Many elements entered into the cause of this failure. The Young Turks proved too young to steer such a gigantic enterprise in its right course. The people of the Empire was a composite of many races of mutually exclusive traditions, religions, languages, and interests. Equality before the law of Christian and Mohammedan could not easily be harmonized with the Moslem *sheriat*. The question of the centralizing and decentralizing of the government of the Empire soon became a vexing problem. The binding of the holy Caliph by a parliamentary law seemed to conservative Mohammedans to do away with the sacredness of his office, and so forth.

One thing, however, seemed reasonably certain. The Young Turks approached their mighty task with good intentions. They had faith in the success of the new movement, and, so far as they knew what they themselves were, they meant to remain loyal to the principles of justice and equality. They had also a firm belief that the great European nations would certainly give every encouragement to so worthy a cause which was in perfect harmony with their own noblest aspirations.

But the Christian nations cold-shouldered the Turkish Revolution. Their approval of it was icily formal. The unification of Turkey as a constitutional monarchy seemed to them to be a check to their own imperialistic 'ambitions. It meant "hands off" the affairs of the "Sick Man of Europe." At any rate, they had "no faith in Turkish declarations and promises." In this they may have been right. But their indifference toward the Young Turks at that time has been condemned as a conspiracy with the Fates, not only against Turkey, but against the peace of Europe, also.

Scarcely had the Young Turks had time enough to get their bearing when in 1911-12, in a most cold-blooded manner, Italy seized the Turkish province of Tripoli. The other European Powers looked on with affected disapproval, but did nothing to check the unprovoked aggression. The Turks cried to Europe for justice, but to no good purpose. A year later, Greece, Serbia, Bulgaria, and Montenegro banded themselves together and attacked Turkey. The declared purpose of the Balkan War was the driving of the Turk out of Europe. Again the great European Powers looked on "pained," but did not interfere on Turkey's behalf. They did at the invitation of England hold the famous Conference of Ambassadors, whose real purpose was to keep the peace among themselves. That Conference issued a declaration to the effect that no annexation of territory would be allowed after the Balkan War, no matter which side won the victory. But that declaration proved only a scrap of paper. The victorious enemies of Turkey did annex her territory to the very suburbs of Constantinople, without even a formal protest from the Great Powers. It was only when the Balkan States turned against one another in the Second Balkan War that the Turks went forth and recaptured Adrianople unopposed.

As may be readily inferred, those shattering events could not fail to make the Young Turks take counsel of their weakness rather than their strength. Their bad qualities came to the fore. Their complete loss of faith in the great European Powers led them also to lose faith in one another and in the non-Turkish elements in the Empire. Of course their original purpose was to "Turkify" all the Sultan's subjects. But that the method they first had in mind was the extermination of the non-Turkish races is utterly unthinkable. They could not conceivably have thought it possible for them to exterminate the millions of Mohammedan Arabs within the Empire, even if they had such a design against the Christians, which I feel certain they did not at first have. Their hope was that by establishing an educational system they would be able to make the Turkish language the language of the country and in process of time teach the various racial elements to think of themselves as Ottomans.

But under the stress of the circumstances mentioned above the Young Turks lost faith in all "enlightened" modern methods. They reverted to a lower type. They re-established the spy system, and became convinced that the non-Turkish elements in the Empire were the instrumentalities of European intrigues. It was then, perhaps, that they thought that the extermination of the Christian population, when opportunity offered itself, would simplify their Turkification programme and enable them to awe the Mohammedan Arabs into submission. It was this plan which they tried to carry out during the World War, especially in Syria and Armenia.

When, in about a year after the Balkan War, the World War broke out, both the Central Powers and the Allies began to woo the Turks. "Come with us, and we will do thee good," was the invitation from either side. The Turks, tortured by their recent experiences, stood as between the devil and the deep sea. "Whither shall we turn?" was their vexing question.

The real reasons why the Turks finally chose to cast their lot with the Central Powers have never been published. What has been known more or less clearly is that the Turkish leaders were not unanimous in their decision; that those among the military men who effected that momentous decision were educated in Germany and had an overpowering vision of the mighty German army; the proximity of Turkey to the Central Powers made any other decision a most perilous adventure. And, finally, the fact that nearly a hundred million Mohammedans were British and French subjects induced the opinion that, in case Turkey lost the war, France and England would be more merciful to the Turks on account of their coreligionists than Germany ever would be.

When it became certain that the Central Powers were doomed to defeat, there was scarcely an intelligent Turk who believed that Turkish rule would survive the conflict. The end had come as a foreordained thing. The only flicker of hope left for the Turks was that Anatolia, whose population was almost wholly Turkish, would be given to them as a place to rule and to die in.

The Turks were not at the Paris Peace Conference in the body, but they were there in the spirit. Their shrewdest statesmen had not forgotten what spirit the great European Powers were of. They could not forget that the rival ambitions of those Powers had kept the Turks for the last two hundred years on the Bosphorus. Though paralyzed by military defeat, they yet hoped that Satan would not on this occasion fail to appear as of yore in the council of their enemies and there play his old game. His Lowness did not fail!

Even before the Paris Conference met, the Allies were torn asunder by internal dissensions. The war had screened all that from the general public, but it was well known to those on the "inside."

The "peace" table proved the chessboard of the old diplomacy. The players approached their game in ill-temper. "To have and to hold" was the overmastering desire of European statesmen. Not only that England, France, Italy, and Greece began to quarrel among themselves over the spoils, but the first two Powers proceeded to rival one another in professing "true friendship" for the Turks. The millions of Mohammedans also under the British and French flags, as the Turks had expected, began to be heard from in behalf of their sacred Caliphate. The center of unity of the Moslem world must not be destroyed. The Turks heard of all this, and thanked Allah and took courage.

It was in the spring of 1919 when, by the authority of the Allies, the Greeks occupied Smyrna in execution of Article 7 of the Armistice, that the historic adventure of Mustepha Kemal Pasha began in Asia Minor. [1]

The Turks, while not loving the Great Powers were always ready to admit their higher civilization, and to recognize them as victors in the war. But they refused to see the Greeks in the same light. For centuries the Greeks had been a despised subject race, tolerated,
useful traders, clerks, and shopkeepers, but essentially inferior. Moreover, they know what had been the Greek's share in the war. To be first disarmed by the Great Powers and then given over to the tender mercies of the Greek rayahs was an intolerable humiliation, and even in their desperate condition they were goaded into resistance.

Before these events a small number of Turks had formed associations for the protection of Turkish rights in Thrace, Smyrna, Cilicia, and Eastern Anatolia the four territories more directly menaced. But until the Greek landing at Smyrna this movement had little support among the masses, who only wanted peace and food.

It was at this moment that Mustepha Kemal Pasha comes on the scene. He had greatly distinguished himself during the war, especially at the Dardanelles, where he commanded a brigade...That event [the Greek landing at Smyrna] induced him to leave Constantinople, nominally to inspect the troops in the Erzerum area, but in reality to organize resistance against the Greek invasion.

Mustepha Kemal's first task was to coordinate the four associations for the defense of Turkish rights. He established himself at Erzerum, the seat of the Eastern association and became the president of it. The Eastern association convened a congress at Erzerum in August, 1919, of delegates from all the Eastern vilayets. In its resolution it renounced all claims to the non-Turkish provinces, but demanded absolute independence for Turkish territories within the armistice line and the expulsion of the Greeks from Smyrna.

The Sultan's Government, presided over by Damad Ferid Pasha, disowned the Nationalist movement as it was called, and ordered Mustepha Kemal to return to Constantinople. On his refusal he was deprived of his rank and declared a rebel. [2]

In addition to this, Mustepha Kemal encountered serious difficulties with his own fellow-Moslems in Asia Minor. Nevertheless, he persisted in his efforts and gradually won the confidence and support of many of the ablest men of his nation.

A number [says the writer just quoted] of the most intelligent men in Turkey - high officials, officers, diplomats, landowners, journalists, etc. - had rallied to Mustepha Kemal's standard, as representing the only chance of saving something of the Turkish nation...His strength lay in the fact that he voiced and embodied the feelings of the immense majority of the nation in their exasperation at having their fairest territories shorn from them and given to the hated Yunan.

In April, 1920, the Supreme Council met at San Remo to prepare the Turkish treaty...The San Remo decisions were embodied in the Sevres Treaty, whereby a territory roughly corresponding to the Greek occupied zone (except Aidin and some other places) was assigned to Greece, under some shadowy limitations in favor of Turkish sovereignty; an undelimited Armenian State was also created. By the so-called "Tripartite Agreement" the other parts of Turkey were divided into a British, a French, and an Italian zone of "economic priority." The treaty was signed, under protest by the Turkish delegates, but no one, except M. Venizelos and perhaps Mr. Lloyd George, believed it would ever be executed.

The Sèvres Treaty, thanks to the Turkish Nationalists and the growing dissensions between its makers, never was executed. The Greek military operations in Asia Minor proved disastrous. The French also found the occupation of Cilicia terribly costly. Their mistrust of England's designs, the unexpectedly strong resistance by the Turkish Nationalists, and a restless Syria in their rear, compelled the French to patch up a separate peace with Mustepha Kemal, and, in order to strengthen him against the Greeks and the British, "sold" to him great quantities of arms and munitions.

Owing also to the success of Turkish propaganda in Afghanistan, Turkestan, India, and other places, the Moslems in those countries were profoundly agitated by the "injustice" done to their Turkish coreligionists and the Caliph of Islam. Because of this, England, with characteristic wisdom and in order to checkmate France, swung to the Turkish side.

At the Near East Conference held in Paris last March, the Turks were conceded almost all their claims, except those to Adrianople and part of Eastern Thrace. They maintain their sovereignty over all Asia Minor and all of the territory bounded by the Caucasus, Persia, Mesopotamia, and the Mediterranean and the Agean Seas. Constantinople remains Turkey's, and she retains Armenia, with the population under the protection of the League of Nations. [3]

The Paris Conference, and the other conferences which grew out of it, not only failed to solve the problems of the Near East, ,but made them graver and more vexatious than ever. Could America by accepting the trust as the protector of Armenia have exerted a tranquillizing influence over the Near East? That was the hope of all of us who went to Paris to plead for the Eastern countries. I wish now that America might assume a share of the responsibility in that part of the world and try more earnestly than she is now doing to hold the Turks in check and to curb the ambitions of European colonizers. But, so far as we knew, with regard to all these problems, America proved helpless at the peace table. The acrid atmosphere of diplomacy compelled Mr. Wilson to "wash his hands clean of the Eastern Question." The question now is, Would America be more successful in dealing with the problems of the Near East while in actual charge of one or more of the Eastern countries, and would she prove more of a match for the seasoned diplomats of Europe than she was at Paris with her hands free and all Europe looking to her for help?

Let American statesmen answer this question.

So far the Turks have been victorious both as diplomats and as fighters. As the earlier chapters of this book are going through the press (early September, 1922) the press dispatches from Asia Minor carrying the news of crushing Turkish victories over the Greek armies are on the first pages of the great newspapers of the world. The smashing blows of Kemal Pasha's armies have definitely eliminated Greece as a factor in Near Eastern affairs. The echoes of the great victory are already causing uprisings among the Mohammedans in other parts of the Near East. It is very reasonable to believe that the irreconcilable dissensions among France, England, and Italy and the growing revolt of the Moslem world against Christian political domination may yet enable the Turks to renew their conquests and regain their lost provinces.

The Turks have been restored to power and they remain Turks. Europe, by being divided against itself, has virtually placed the knife once more in the Turk's hand, and Europe, together with the unfortunate non-Turkish elements in Turkey, will in course of time reap the evil consequences.

[1] The following quotations are taken from the *Edinburgh Review*, January, 1922, from an article entitled "The Problem of Asia Minor," and signed "Adalia."
[2] Later revelations have made it almost certain that Mustepha Kemal and the Sultan's Government always were in perfect accord. Constantinople being in the hands of the Allies no such movement as that of the Nationalists could be organized in it. Asia Minor was the only region in the Empire where the Turks could make their last stand.
[3] From an Associated Press dispatch in the *Boston Transcript*, March 27, 1922.

Chapter Twenty-One - Zionism A New Eastern Problem

THE present contention between the people of Palestine and the Zionists is one of the most deplorable aspects of the troubled life of the Holy Land; and if the political programme of Zionism is finally carried out, the event may be counted one of the saddest tragedies in the history of Palestine and in the history of the Jews.

When one thinks of the many centuries - from the time of the Arabian conquest of Palestine to the World War - during which the Jews and the non-Jews of that country lived at peace with one another, one is dismayed to realize that the recent intrusion of alien forces has stirred such enmities in Palestine, whose fire seems to be unquenchable. The non-Jews, who for these many centuries have been in the majority, had always looked upon the Jewish minority as neighbors and fellow subjects of the ruling power. The quarrels between the Jews and the non-Jews never had been of greater intensity than those which often occur between the various sects, or the various clans of the same faith, in Eastern countries. The Jews of Palestine have never had to undergo such persecutions as many of their coreligionists have suffered in certain parts of Europe. No pogroms have ever taken place in the Holy Land.

The Zionists, also, who had been coming into Palestine for years previous to the war, were left absolutely unmolested. More than thirty years ago I used to hear in my Lebanon home of Zionist immigration to the Holy Land. So far as I remember, those immigrants were looked upon by the people of the country as peaceful, industrious Jews who had come in as home-seekers, with no political designs whatever. The Moslems, even though they were under a ruler of their own faith who was bound by the Koran to protect them at whatever cost, never demanded from the Sultan the expulsion of the Zionists. More than thirty Zionist colonies existed in Palestine before the war, which the non-Jews considered as legitimate enterprises. The only thing which I remember used to be said about those Zionists was that they did not seem overly scrupulous in regarding the rights of their non-Jewish neighbors; but even then it was thought that time would correct such a defect. The Zionists might have continued to come into Palestine as home-seekers and as industrial workers, unopposed, but for the recent political programme of Zionism whose working-out would mean the ultimate subjugation by the Zionists of the non-Jewish elements.

So the revolt of the people of Palestine against Zionism, as may readily be seen, is neither racial nor religious. It is an instinctive reaction against an invasion which threatens their social and political existence. Self-preservation is their driving motive. It is not an uprising against the Zionists simply because they are Jews. I am very certain that if the Armenians, for an example, were to come into Palestine with the purpose of making of it an Armenian State, the resistance of the Palestinians to them would be no less determined. The case is elementary. When a problem arising out of the necessities of a country's own life confronts its people, they accept it and deal with it calmly as a natural difficulty. But when a problem is forced upon an unoffending country by a superior power, the people of that country are bound to look upon it, to use a Biblical phrase, as an accursed thing to which no community can honorably reconcile itself.

Political Zionism is being forced upon Palestine by a group of Zionist idealists, backed up by British military power. The offense is utterly unprovoked. The leaders of this movement have chosen to carry on an experiment in colonization at the expense of the present owners of Palestine, and the British Government is supporting the enterprise for a purpose of its own vitally related to Great Britain's intricate policy in the East. This problem needs to be studied with perfect freedom from religious and racial prejudice. It is a political problem, and the cry of the people of Palestine against it is for justice and fair play. Let us therefore face the facts.

In the preceding chapters we have seen how, first, in the Kitchener Agreement with King Husein, Great Britain acknowledged the independence of the Arab countries, of which Palestine is an integral part, and, second, in 1918, in a joint declaration the British and the French solemnly promised to guarantee to those Eastern countries "the establishment of governments and administrations *deriving their authority from the initiative and free choice of the native population.*" The people of Palestine, like their fellow-Syrians, hailed these declarations as the charter of their freedom and gave the British arms in the Eastern campaign all possible support. Palestine, as the students of history know, is a province of Syria to which it was annexed by the Romans shortly before the Christian era. [1] The expectation was that after the war Syria would become a federation of autonomous provinces of which Palestine, of course, would be a member.

Now, it can easily be imagined with what dismay the people of Syria in general and of Palestine in particular received the Balfour Declaration promising Palestine to the Zionists together with British aid to enable them to establish in that land a Jewish state. When during the war the Arab army and afflicted Syria were engaged in facilitating General Allenby's advance against the Turks, the Zionists were busy perfecting their designs against Palestine. They virtually held up the British Government at a most critical time in the war and succeeded in making their cause seem the desire of the fourteen million Jews in the world. The British Government, in a most unwarrantable manner and contrary to the letter and spirit of its treaty with the Arabs, and its later declaration to the peoples of the "Eastern countries," concluded agreements with the Zionists most detrimental to the people of Palestine, without ever permitting them to be heard in their own behalf. The first thing they knew was that Palestine was arbitrarily detached from Syria and practically handed over to the Zionists. The Balfour Declaration was as follows:

His Majesty's Government view with favour the establishment in Palestine of a National Home for the Jewish people and will use their best endeavours to facilitate the achievement of this object: it being clearly understood that nothing shall be done which may prejudice the civil and religious rights of existing non-Jewish communities in Palestine or the rights and political status enjoyed by Jews in any other country.

Whatever the necessities of the war and their future designs in the East may have led the British Government cautiously to promise the Zionists, to these Palestine seemed a defenseless prey.

In Palestine itself the people whose national home it already was took quite another view. They were still under the Turks, from whom they first heard of it. It was, to use their own phrase, a bolt from the blue, and they were thoroughly alarmed at the economic difficulty of two national homes in one house. Their great ambition was the promised independence, and, notwithstanding Turkish taunts, they refused to believe that the British would not keep their word. This was their attitude at the beginning of the occupation, but a few months later, when a Zionist commission under the leadership of Dr. Weizmann arrived in Palestine, they began to be seriously perturbed. This commission, under instructions from His Majesty's Government, was accorded a semi-official status to "act as an advisory body to the British authorities in Palestine in all matters relating to Jews, or which may affect the establishment of a National Home for the Jewish people in accordance with the Declaration of His Majesty's Government." To this Zionist commission a British officer, Major the Hon. W. Ormsby-Gore, M.P., was attached as political officer, and to it were given a number of special privileges, such as railway and customs facilities, which no one else had. Its influential connections in England, which it made the most of, exaggerated its importance in the eyes of General Allenby's staff officers, inexperienced as they were in dealing with politics and politicians. [2]

Such were the early and carefully guarded machinations of the Zionist leaders in England. Their cause was, and has been since, so presented through the instrumentality of a friendly press as to seem worthy of the sympathy and support of the whole world. When asked whether their purpose is to take the reins of government in Palestine into their own hands they answer, "No, not now." Not now! But they expect by the unnatural stimulation of Zionist .immigration to Palestine, soon to swamp or drive out the native population and "possess the land." Their attitude may be illustrated as follows: You have a house which has been in your family for generations. Presently a visitor comes and says to you, "In the remote past one of my ancestors lived in this house. Now, I do not intend to take it away from you, but I would like to establish a home in it side by side with you, without in the least interfering with your personal rights. But I have many relatives who are coming here also. In case they should come in large numbers, then, I regret to say, you would have to surrender the whole house to us, for it originally belonged to our clan." It is this "peaceful" invasion that the Palestinians are resisting, and not a well-regulated, non-political Zionist immigration.

Nor do they object to having their country under a British mandate, [3] but they do strenuously object to having the Mandatory Power give their country to another people. Such a Power is not expected utterly to disregard the wishes and interests of the people it is supposed to train in self-government, but to give those wishes a "principal consideration." The demands of the native population are for equality of privilege under the mandatory stipulations of the Covenant of the League of Nations, which regards the opinion of the majority. Here are those fair and just demands which were long ago presented to the British Government:

(1) The formation of a Palestine National Government, responsible, with the advice of a British High Commissioner, to a "parliament elected by those inhabitants of Palestine who lived there before the war, Moslem, Christian, and Jewish."

(2) The abandonment of the present partisan Zionist policy.

(3) The regulation and control of immigration, in accordance with the capacity of the country, by the National Government itself.

(4) The freedom of the Holy Places, which should be left in the custody of their present guardians, from any interference by the National Parliament or any other external authority.

(5) The creation of a local force for internal purposes, subject to and at the expense of the National Government, without any imposition of British regular troops, save if and when required for imperial defense.

Can any fair-minded person detect a taint of injustice in these demands which give equality of privilege and responsibility to all the actual and legitimate owners of Palestine, "Moslems, Christians, and Jews"? And can any such person fail to see the injustice of giving at the very beginning such special privileges to the Zionists and of making one of their leaders the first Governor of Palestine under the mandate? In this manner the people of the country are being practically prevented from exercising their governmental functions until a Zionist majority has been imported from every country of disorganized and Bolshevik Eastern Europe. The present population of Palestine numbers about 700,000, only 70,000 of whom are Jews, and many of these are opposed to Zionism. If Palestine is to be detached from Syria and made a sovereign state, according to what code of justice are its people denied the right to say how their country shall be governed and whether it really belongs to them or to a people which is yet to be imported into it?

The claim by the Zionists of the right to possess Palestine, because in the remote past their ancestors owned it, is a very novel one. According to such logic the Finns might claim Russia; the Arabs, Spain; the Danes, England; and the Indians, America.

Historically Palestine belongs to its present inhabitants. The claim that, because the Jews of more than two thousand years ago owned a part of that country, it should now be given to the present Jews, does not so much confirm as it outrages history. The ancient Jews dispossessed the Jebusites and Canaanites; the Greeks, and after them the Romans, dispossessed the Jews; the Arabs in turn dispossessed the Romans and have owned Palestine for more than twelve hundred years. Would it not be as illogical to give Palestine to the Italians of to-day because their Roman ancestors once possessed it, ruled it for about eight hundred years, and built in it their palaces and temples, as to give it to the Zionists? There are also in Palestine to-day descendants of the ancient nations whom the Hebrews conquered, but failed to exterminate. Let me quote on this point a noted American Orientalist: [4]

Much has been written upon the historic claims of the Jews to this territory, which they held for less than five hundred years, prior to two thousand five hundred years ago. But how about the claims of the Palestinian, who possessed the land before the Jew, and who is still in possession, having lived there for over five thousand years? The Aramaeans, who came from Aram, whom we call Hebrews, under Joshua conquered, and even ruthlessly exterminated, the people of a portion of Palestine; and later on, under David and Solomon, extended their rule over the whole country. But, if we are to decide the question of actual ownership of the territory, the Palestinian who has continually lived there surely has a clearer title than the Jew. Moreover, this decision is based upon the records handed down by the Jew himself. Even the Hebrew language, which the Jews are attempting to revive as their spoken tongue, originally belonged to the people they are trying to oust. The language in Aram-Abraham's ancestral home - was Aramaean; when the Aramaeans came to Palestine, they adopted the Canaanite language, now called Hebrew.

Again the present great shrines of the Holy Land are Christian and Mohammedan, and not Jewish. The Church of the Holy Sepulcher in Jerusalem, the Church of the Nativity in Bethlehem, Gethsemane, Olivet, Bethany, the Jordan, Nazareth, and other sacred places are the shrines of Christendom. The Mosque of Omar, which occupies the area of the ancient temple in Jerusalem, the Mosque of Al-Aksa, Hebron, and other less conspicuous places are Mohammedan shrines. These shrines together command the reverence of eight hundred millions of Christians and Mohammedans. Would it be conducive to the peace of the world to put such holy places under Zionist control? Would that contribute to future Jewish tranquillity and happiness in the East?

Palestine is a small country which cannot possibly sustain comfortably, according to a decent standard of living, a much greater population than that which the natural increase of its present inhabitants will create. The expectation that such a strip of land can provide an outlet for the fourteen million Jews in the world and provide them with a "national home" is sheer folly. Those who know Palestine know this to be true.

The truth is that Palestine cannot support a large population in prosperity. It has a lean and niggardly soil. It is a land of rocky hills, upon which for many centuries a hardy people have survived only with difficulty by cultivating a few patches of soil here and there, with the olive, the fig, citrus fruits, and the grape; or have barely sustained their flocks upon the sparse native vegetation. The streams are few and small, entirely insufficient for the great irrigation system that would be necessary for the general cultivation of the land. The underground sources of water can only be developed at a prodigious capital expense. There are thirteen million Jews in the world; the Zionist organization itself only claims for Palestine a maximum possible population of five millions. Even this claim is on the face of it an extravagant overestimate. After careful study on the spot in Palestine, I prophesy that it will not support more than one million additional inhabitants...

This is the condition of Palestine: not only must agriculture be pursued under the greatest possible handicaps of soil and water, but it is subject to the direct competition of far more favored lands in the very agricultural products for which it is distinctive. These are the citrus fruits, almonds, figs and dates, grapes and wine. How can little Palestine compete in these products with Italy, France, and Spain, and their North African colonies, whose richer soil lies in the direct line of the great march of commerce?

A great industrial Palestine is equally unthinkable. It lacks the raw materials of coal and iron; it lacks the skill in technical processes and the experience in the arts; and, above all, it is not in the path of modern trade currents. What hope is there for Palestine, as an industrial nation, in competition with America, Great Britain, and Germany, with their prodigious resources, their highly organized factories, their great mass-production, and their superb means of transportation? The notion is preposterous. [5]

How under such circumstances can the people of Palestine be expected to acquiesce in a scheme which threatens to make the struggle for existence for them and their children so severe? The little country can be made to produce more than it now does, and that was what its present owners expected to do after their emancipation from Turkish rule. Like all forward-looking communities they had hoped that, as soon as the post-war conditions permitted, they themselves, with European expert aid, would give their country such a development, and not a host of foreign invaders. They were and are now willing to open their gates to normal immigration regulated by their National Government and the capacity of the country. It can be easily realized here that, while to its leaders, and to the outsiders who have not studied the subject in all its phases, Zionism is an enchanting romantic adventure, to the owners of Palestine it is a matter of life and death. It has been injected into the life of that much-afflicted East as a baffling problem for both the Jews and the non-Jews. It is not only Palestine which fears its consequences, but the whole of Syria and Mesapotamia. The other Arabic-speaking countries also realize with no little anxiety that, sooner or later, because of its bearing on the future course of events in Syria, this problem is bound to become also their problem. I have not met a single Easterner who did not profoundly deplore this movement as a great danger to both of the factions which it involves. The revolt against it is deep and strong, and it threatens to continue until the cause is removed.

As has already been stated, the revolt against Zionism is neither racial nor religious. Yet there is a religious side to it which cannot be overlooked in this discussion. It is related to the idea that the Scriptures prophesy the "restoration" of the Jews to Palestine as a precursor of the coming of Christ's kingdom. This erroneous interpretation of certain Bible passages has been completely rejected by modern Biblical scholarship. Those hopes of the "regathering" of Israel were born under the stress of the events which the Exile brought about. They were the hopes of a people which longed for the reestablishment of their political unity under a Jewish king, and not under Jesus of Nazareth. Yet, when King Cyrus issued his historic decree permitting the Jews to return from their captivity to Palestine, only a small number improved the privilege. The Jerusalem which these rebuilt was a mere shadow of that city's ancient glory. Again, when Jesus appeared and sought to gather his people "as a hen gathereth her brood under her wings," only a few Jews followed him, and these" were considered outcasts by their own people.

What would the restoration of the Jews to Palestine mean to-day? Many Christians believe that it would mean a preparation for the second coming of Christ. But this is not what the orthodox Jews expect. To them there has been no *first* coming of Christ. *Their* Messiah is yet to come. The One who came and was summarily rejected by the Jews was not to them the true Messiah. The Messiah whom they expect is one who shall make them rulers over the nations, Christians and all. And what would be the theology of the restored Jews? Certainly not that of the liberals among them upon whom they look as the Roman Catholics look upon the Unitarians. The liberal Jews whose attitude toward Jesus is growing more and more friendly are not the ones who are looking forward to the restoration of the Jews to Palestine, nor would they be accepted by the vast majority of their people as their spokesmen. So, if a few hundred thousand Zionists were finally established in Palestine and called "a restored Israel," notwithstanding the fact that the millions of Jewry would remain outside that little country, the "restoration" would not be a preparation for the coming of Christ's kingdom, but a reestablishment of the very legalism which He rejected while on earth, and whose adherents led Him to the cross. The orthodox Jew who is loyal to his faith can at best only think of Jesus as a youth who had a mistaken idea of his mission.

It is indeed most strange that Christians of the twentieth century, who are crying for international concord and peace on earth for all nations and peoples, should hold the view that God chooses a certain people and neglects all the rest. That His divine plan is restricted by the limits of a tribal religion and His love bounded by the narrow human view of an arbitrary favoritism. To God there can be no Jew and Gentile. The Jews are His children; so also are the Anglo-Saxons, the Celts, the Latins, and every people under His wide heaven. The ancient monarchical idea of favoritism runs counter to Christ's spirit of universal love and to the spirit of democracy and human brotherhood. And what is strange in this connection is that those Christians who hold this idea of a "chosen race" and are willing to give Palestine to the Zionists are not always so willing to have the Jews for their neighbors.

Perhaps no greater injustice can be done to the Jew than to lead him back to Palestine as an invader. The establishment of a Jewish state in Palestine cannot possibly fail to set all the peoples of Western Asia against the Jew and awaken around him the religious and racial hatred of all the past. Had the negotiations of Zionist immigration to Palestine been carried on between a free Syrian Government and the Jews, it is possible that a plan satisfactory to both parties could have been devised. Had the Zionist invaded Palestine as a military force, the sword would have decided the future course of events for the invader and the invaded. In either case the decision would have been such as free and brave men make either at the council table or on the field of battle. But in the present instance the scheme of conquest is most inglorious. It was made in the dark. The people of Palestine had no knowledge of it. The Zionists are coming into the country neither as military invaders with flying banners nor as invited friends. The British forces are holding the Palestinians by the throat, as it were, while the Zionists are creeping in with a grin of derision.

How long can a self-respecting people endure such a state of things? How long will Great Britain, with a restless India, an emancipated Egypt, and a Moslem world in revolt, be able to afford the Zionists such protection? The leaders of the Zionists have been able by various means to induce many of the politicians and statesmen of Europe and America to approve their plans. Even the American Congress has granted them its endorsement. But what will all that come to? England, for an example, succeeded at the Paris Conference in obtaining recognition of her annexation of Egypt during the war. The United States Government also granted such a recognition. What did all that amount to? Nothing. The people of Egypt kept up the struggle for the freedom of their country until they secured it. Very recently the United States Government, which had recognized England's "right" to annex Egypt to her Empire, has had to recognize the King of Egypt as an independent sovereign. So it will be some day in Palestine. It is not conceivable that Great Britain, or the League of Nations, or America, will send soldiers to shoot down the Palestinians in order to enable the Zionists to carry out their designs. The whole Moslem world is opposed to Zionism, and with that world the traffickers with the fortunes of the Holy Land will have to reckon.

And is there any conceivable reason why England should fight the battles of the Jews against the Syrians and the Arabs? Says Hilaire Belloc:

If there were any reason to suppose a natural alliance between the British Army and the Jews; if we could imagine British officers and men taking a natural pleasure in ousting the Arab and making way for the Jew, it would be another matter. If there were something in the nature of things which made that alliance permanent and stable, if the Jews were a fully accepted part of the British Commonwealth as are, for instance, the Scots or the Welsh, some permanent arrangement might be possible. But they are nothing of the sort. The position is wholly unnatural. It cannot last. And if it cannot last with the British connection, how should it last with any other? How shall the transition be made from a British protectorate to another protectorate? Or how, seeing what violent hatreds have already been roused by the mere beginnings of the experiment, shall the conflict which makes the protectorate necessary be avoided?

So far the dislike of the position, which is very far-reaching, and already very deep in England, is a passive dislike. No English soldier has yet been killed; there has been but little necessity, as yet, to repress the Arab and create hostility, though even what little necessity there has been has been so odious to the troops concerned. But things cannot remain in that state. The conflict is inevitable. When the conflict comes the feeling which has hitherto been passive will become active. People will not tolerate the loss of sons and brothers in a quarrel which is not theirs, which cannot possibly strengthen the British State; which, if anything, must weaken it; which is felt to be precarious and ephemeral, and which will be undertaken against those with whom British sympathy naturally lies, and in favor of those with whom the average soldier and citizen - unlike the professional politician - has no ties and no sympathy. [6]

If the Zionist movement, which Mr. Morgenthau has characterized as "the most stupendous fallacy in Jewish history," had the real promise of improving the lot of the oppressed Jews in the world, one would say that the protests of the people of Palestine might be ignored in favor of a scheme whose success would mean the solution of one of the world's greatest problems. But Zionism is a dream whose realization would only create another serious problem for Western Asia and a worse problem for the Jews. Ultimately the Jews themselves would have to pay the frightful cost of this aggression.

Those politicians, orators, and visionaries, who are far away from the scene and who risk nothing themselves in supporting Zionism but an effusion of words, should realize that it is a condition here and not a theory which we have to deal with. They should understand that Zionism as an ideal spiritual community is vastly different from Zionism as a scheme of political and economic conquest; that while the one is a state of mind which concerns only those who believe in it, the other is an act of aggression against an innocent people, which threatens to fill the future with horror; that to support such a scheme of conquest does not mean to lessen, but to multiply, the miseries of the "oppressed Jews," and to compel the people of the Holy Land to expend in self-defense the powers and the treasure which they should expend in self-development.

The latest phase of the Palestinian question up to the present (September 1, 1922) has been the approval, by the Council of the League of Nations, of the mandates for Syria and Palestine. It will be remembered that those mandates were created at the Paris Peace Conference by the very Powers who had divided those Eastern countries between them, with utter disregard for the wishes of the inhabitants. Those same powers control the Council of the League. France was "anxious that the mandates should be accepted immediately," in order to secure sanction for her occupation of Syria against the wishes of the large majority of the Syrian people. So was England also anxious to have the Palestinian mandate settled, "in order to allay the agitation and unrest among the different racial elements in the mandate areas." Italy finally acquiesced in the matter in consideration of the conservation of her own interests in other parts of the Near East. Consequently the Council of the League approved the mandates.

The result of this cryptic transaction, however, has been different from that which was expected. The unrest in Syria and Palestine has greatly increased. The peoples there violently object to having their fate sealed in this manner and without their consent.

But from the side of the British Government a new interpretation has been given the Balfour Declaration, to the effect that Palestine "cannot be a distinctly Jewish state, although Jews may remain or go into the country as of right and not of sufferance." This altogether unnecessary declaration seems to have been sent out as a feeler to induce fresh reactions from both the Palestinians and the Zionists. It has, however, exerted no soothing influence. The Palestinians cannot see why Great Britain should be partial to either side in the controversy.

As yet this threatening issue has not passed the state of a peaceful settlement. It is still within the power of Great Britain and the League of Nations to spare the East the pains and horrors of a new racial and political conflict. Britain's promise to the Zionist of a land which belongs to another people should be recalled. The League of Nations should insist on the carrying-out of the terms of the mandate for Palestine in the interest of its present and rightful owners. A native Palestinian Government should be established on the basis of representation proportionate to the number of Moslems, Christians, and Jews. Then negotiations concerning Zionist immigration to Palestine might be undertaken with that Government without coercion by an alien military power. Under such circumstances Jewish educational and industrial enterprises would not be excluded from Palestine. The Zionists, like other immigrants, could then come in in such numbers as the capacity of the country would permit, and the Jews and the non-Jews would live together in that historic land as fellow-workers for a common cause and as heirs of peace.

[1] The current custom of saying "Syria *and* Palestine" follows the Bible usage, and goes back to the time when the region now known as Syria contained numerous small kingdoms. In Syrian the saying "Syria and Palestine" is like saying "the United States and Texas."
[2] From Vivian Gabriel's article in the *Edinburgh Review,* quoted above.
[3] More recent developments in Palestine indicate that the persistence of the British authorities in their partiality to the Zionists is turning the people of the country against the mandate idea.
[4] Albert T. Clay, Professor of Assyriology and Babylonian Literature at Yale, in an article entitled "Political Zionism," the *Atlantic Monthly,* February, 1921.
[5] "Zionism a Surrender, Not a Solution," by Henry Morgenthau, in *The World's Work,* July, 1921.
[6] *The Jews.* (Houghton Mifflin Company.)

Chapter Twenty-Two - The Spirit over the Chaos

OUR comparative study of the East and the West and our review of recent events and present conditions in Asiatic countries, brief as they have been, have, I trust, made clear a few facts of very vital importance. We have seen that the Eastern mind and the Western mind diverge so widely that any attempt to force them into a unity is foredoomed to failure. Whatever may have happened in the remote past, when the human species was still plastic and very sensitive to formative influences, is of the past. Prehistoric man is not the type we have to deal with to-day. The races of men whom we know at present as nations and peoples are types which centuries of evolution have shaped and hardened, and which no hasty human processes can create or annul. The voluntary gathering of racial elements together in one country, like America, and the voluntary submission to new influences, may in the process of time evolve a human composite called a people with general characteristics strong enough to vouchsafe for it a peaceful and harmonious existence. Yet even here the fusion of such elements is creating staggering problems; and the success attained is the result of the constant elimination of the "newcomer" and the exclusion of the racial idea from the mind of his offspring. In other words, the new influences are not changing the old stock, but killing it, and replacing it by a new breed. However, what may be accomplished in the case of individuals transplanted to a new environment and subjected to new training cannot be accomplished in the case of a people attached to their native soil and governed by their own racial traditions. If the West means to convert the East to its own ways of thinking and living, and if its purpose is to rule the East according to Western methods, then the outcome of the mighty struggle must inevitably be the destruction of either the invaded or the invader.

We have seen also in the light of recent developments that the East is no longer the submissive world it has been thought to be for centuries. It is being spurred to resistance and defiance seemingly by a power higher than itself. The West also has placed in the hands of the East weapons which this ancient world means to use in defense of its life and institutions.

Furthermore, the rivalries of the European Powers in Asia, especially during the last hundred years, have been the chief disturbers of the peace of the world. For each one of those Powers the "Star of Empire" has been moving East. The position of Great Britain in India has been to the other Great Powers of Europe an exasperating point of vantage. Great Britain's policy in dealing with Turkey, and more recently with Japan, Russia, and Persia, has been based on her interest in India. Germany's mad war designs from which the whole world is now suffering were in no small way conditioned by the policies of her rivals in Asia. Her scheme of the Berlin-Constantinople-Bagdad Railway was meant to destroy the security of the British position in India and to weaken Great Britain's hold upon Persia., Russia, France, and Italy - England's friends - would under no circumstances allow the Mediterranean to become an "English lake." In fact the major causes of the greatest diplomatic and military conflicts in Europe for the last hundred years have been the colonizing designs of the European nations in the East. Nor have such designs been relegated to the past. Even at this time in which I write, England and France are racing with each other for the control of the Arab world. France is exerting every effort to win to her side Ben-Saud, the ruler of Nedjid, and to strengthen him against King Husein of Hedjaz, who is an ally of the British, and against King Feisal of Irak, France's enemy. Now the Arab world more than the Turkish world is the arena of European diplomacy.

Meantime the Eastern countries have to pay the piper. Those long-suffering countries are being transferred in the councils of Europe from one Power to another, much like feudal estates. The people are being sold with the land and forced to acquiesce in the transaction. But the Asiatic peoples are not like the savage tribes of certain African regions. Their aspirations are those of civilized men, and their achievements in history, as has been stated, are among the great glories of the human race. The present state of European civilization does not tend to convince the Easterners that it would be alto-gether a blessing for them to have such a civilization forced upon them with all its militaristic and anarchistic tendencies. The only Western country in which all of them have confidence is America. They would have her as a dis-interested teacher and guide; but America is not in a position to undertake the great philanthropic mission.

In sum, our review of the relations of Europe with the East has revealed the sad fact that the confidence of the Easterners in their European "civiliz-ers" has been destroyed. Asia is in a state of genuine revolt against Western domination. Greed, avarice, and force, have done their destructive work. Is there no way in which Good Will can be given an opportunity to exercise its healing functions?

The East and the West have a common spiritual heritage. The latter has received from the former its noblest religious precepts and joined to them its own great hopes and aspirations. In both these worlds it is conceded that all greatness, all culture, all progress, and whatever tends to promote peace and happiness in the world, are in the end spiritual. And we find to-day that the problems which vex the world and disturb its peace are not so much intellec-tual and economic, as they are moral, problems. The world is unspeakably rich in thought and material possessions, but spiritually is on the verge of bankruptcy. It already has enough material wealth comfortably to feed, clothe, and house every member of the human family, and to allot to each not a few luxuries. Our one need, therefore, is to realize that, with this vast en-largement of the intellect and the body, we must have a corresponding en-largement of soul, if we are not to perish fighting.

The ancient story of the creation in our Scripture is more a psalm of adora-tion than a historical document. Yet that primitive poetic narrative contains a thought which the present age would do well to ponder. That the ancient writer, whoever he was, puts the creation of vegetation before the creation of the sun matters little. His real gift which is of immortal worth to the world is to be found in his saying, "And the Spirit of God moved upon the face of the waters." Over the tumultuous shapelessness of primitive matter the good Spirit brooded as a fashioner of worlds. The Eternal Yea overshadowed the chaos. Out of its darkness it called the shining stars and out of its lifelessness the myriads of living forms. Because of the brooding of the good Spirit over it, the chaos culminated in man.

Emerson alludes to this in one of his choicest utterances. "As the world," says the Concord seer, "was plastic and fluid in the hands of God, so it remains to so much of his attributes as we bring to it. To ignorance and sin it is flint."

This has been the declaration of deep-visioned seers in every human crisis, and the truth of it is amply borne out by experience. In the last analysis men's gravest problems are moral problems. They are the symptoms of moral chaos. It is well to focus upon these problems human skill and ingenuity. But in this realm only the good Spirit or the Spirit of Good Will can bring order out of chaos. To mere human cunning the world is flint. To spirit, to the normal and healthy functioning of life, the world is always plastic and ready to be refashioned. The living seed plays with matter. It takes it up and reshapes it according to the seed's own design. It makes it fulfill a higher law. Matter gives itself up when it comes in touch with life. Its hardness and dullness are then converted into flexibility and beauty.

So also do matter and life respond to the constructive mind. At the touch of beneficent genius, the wilderness becomes a garden. At the call of the artist, the granite and marble strata rise from their cold beds and are grouped together in the forms of palaces, forums, and temples. They assume human forms and become inspiring companions.

The same law obtains also in the moral realm. A spiritual genius changes the course of history. The world is never the same after his advent as it was before. Such a seer reasserts the dominance of the creative spirit and causes it again to hover over the deeps of a disordered world as a divine architect. "To this event the ages ran." Beneficent intentions on the part of statesmen and scholars are the urgent demand of every age. All engineering in the world of matter and of mind must be made subject to the good Spirit. It must be brought to bear on the various possibilities of life and given free scope to bring order out of chaos and articulate forms out of formlessness.

To ignorance and sin the world is flint. To fear, selfishness, envy, and indifference nature is a stubborn impossibility. Only chaos can follow such attitudes. To the spiritual hero the world is neither an accident nor an irredeemable evil, but is ready to respond to genius, courage, high purpose.

There is no social problem which a community of spiritually minded men and nations cannot solve. What are "troubled times" but the condition of men and women who have lost sight of supreme moral values? What are "hard times" but the results of human greed and human improvidence? What is war but the loathsome offspring of human hatred? With such motives chaos ceases to be the realm of unrealized possibilities and becomes an abyss of despair.

Men and nations can be friends if they will However, "not by might nor by power, but by my spirit, saith the Lord." When statesmen meet for the purpose of outwitting and deceiving one another, as they have done at the historic "peace" conferences, the world for them becomes flint. When they create and mature designs to exploit the weaker peoples of the earth and extend their own "spheres of influence," then tribulation and anguish sooner or later beset their way. Why, for an example, should there be a "future war" between the Asiatic and the European nations? Is it because of lack of "production" and of technical skill? No! It is because of a mutual lack of confidence. The Eastern nations have become convinced that the Western nations are their despoilers, and not their friends. If there is to be any "engineering" to better the relations between these peoples, Good Will must be the chief engineer. We are seeking to-day to establish a League of Nations and to develop an "international mind." These are, indeed, consummations devoutly to be wished. But let us remember that the quality of "the international mind" is always that of the collective qualities of the national minds of which it consists. It can be "international" and still be very bad. The peoples of the world can have no international social order better than themselves. The larger the number of avaricious citizens, the greater and darker the national and the international chaos. To such the world is flint. Only the good Spirit can bring order out of chaos and set great luminaries of hope in the social firmament.

It is one of the most amazing aspects of human life that the great nations, whose altars shine with the light of a religion whose first words are Love and Redemption, so seldom allow that ineffable ray to penetrate into their diplomatic councils. In those councils might is right; the strong is the despoiler of the weak. With such axioms as the basis for action, the conquests of Asia by Europe have been carried on for generations. The results, however, have been a warning and not an encouragement to the invaders. The fruits have been blood and fire, and not prosperity and peace. The signs are not lacking that, under the leadership of an Asiatic nation like Japan, on the one hand, and a united Moslem world, on the other, the tide of conquest may before many decades run from east to west.

With utter disregard of the fact that up to this time their efforts along this line have been a failure, the Western nations are still of the opinion that they must "reform" the Eastern peoples by conquest and alien rule. They would Westernize the East. The Easterners, however, do not wish to be Westernized. Even if the leopard would, he could not change his spots. True, there are to-day many Eastern families who wear the externals of European civilization. They are attired in European-made garments, they use knives and forks in eating, they speak European languages, and even have afternoon teas, but they are exceptions to the rule. Furthermore, their souls remain Oriental to their very depths, and their real character is only faintly revealed by their newly acquired habits. They do not seem "genuine" either to the East or to the West. The real peoples of the East would gladly become better Orientals, but they instinctively and definitely refuse to become the puppets of an "imported and bastard civilization." They very clearly see also that the real object of their invaders from the West is not the creation of a new type of man in the East, but the opening of new markets. They have always welcomed and respected the disinterested Western educator in their midst, although the convert-seeking missionary has always seemed to those deeply religious peoples to be rather a superfluity. The enlightened among them have always hoped that education would in course of time reform for them their own religion. They remained trustful of such Western altruism, until the designs of European diplomats convinced those Easterners that the Western educator in their midst was the forerunner of the colonizing soldier. Was not this the very thing which the eminent Frenchman quoted above intimated to me in Paris when he said that the French would control Syria because their schools have been in that country for many generations?

The enlightened Easterners at home, and those of us in the West who are of Eastern nativity and Western training, realize that Eastern civilization needs to be renewed and reconstructed. We realize, also, that much of the material for such reconstruction must by necessity be borrowed from the West. The Easterners need to become more aggressive and resolute in dealing with the material, aesthetic, and educational phases of their civilization. They need to have cleaner cities, a larger intellectual environment, greater regard for law and order, more efficient means of communication, and more of the feminine influence in their social life. We love to think of a new East coming into being by the help of the West, but without the irritating thought of the "colonizer" and the "colonized," the "alien ruler" and the "native subjects." Under such conditions the East will remain the East, but will become a better East, and the West, by supplying the many needs of the East, which itself could not supply for some time to come, will *peaceably* have the coveted "markets" for both its genius and its wares.

To this end there must be many points of contact between the East and the West. But it is very essential that the borrower and the lender should first of all be cooperative friends. The agencies of contacts between those two worlds must be friendly intercourse and amorous spiritual interpenetration, and not the creeping tentacles of the invader. Whatever the East may have to borrow of Western thought must be translated in transmission in order that it may do its beneficent work. Like poetry, when translated from one language into another, the thought of the West must be translated to the East according to the spirit, and not the letter. The East should be allowed to borrow from the West on the East's own terms. Its own thinkers and wise men must be its mediums of transmission and agencies of transformation. They must not receive Western thought as they would merchandise, but absorb, so far as may be desirable, the spirit of the West and re-express it to the East in its own forms of thought. Only in this way can the East distil wisdom from Western civilization and assimilate it into character. If it is to be of significant value to either the East or the West, a new Eastern civilization must be genuinely Eastern. It must not be a replica of Western civilization, which itself needs a hundred reforms, but must be born of the East's own spiritual, believing, long-suffering soul. If Eastern governments do not become exactly Western in form; if Eastern cities do not become roaring industrial furnaces, and are not afflicted with such corporeality as that of New York, Chicago, and London; if the Easterners do not learn to desert their churches on the Sabbath for the country club and the golf links, because of the drain business makes upon their vitality during the week; and if they do not change the fashion of their garments every season, and eat to a reprehensible satiety, simply because they are financially prosperous - if the Easterners do not adopt quite all such features of "modern civilization," the world would be much the richer for it. We do not want the Easterner ever to believe that, after he has changed his agricultural life into an industrial life, and forsaken his seat under his own vine and fig tree, with their fragrant shade and beckoning fruit, for an iron and cement bench in a "municipal park," he has become civilized. If he can secure from the West the Anglo-Saxon's veracity and his love of liberty and law without his haughtiness and inordinate commercialism: if he can acquire the Latin's artistic qualities without his inflammable temperament and excessive "personal liberty," and the Teuton's efficiency and thoroughness without his materialism and lust for power and dominion, then the contact of the Easterner with the West will be immensely profitable. Otherwise, I believe that a slower progress urged by his own genius would be far better for him. Better for him to bear the ills with which he is familiar than to fly to those he knows not of.

The Oriental must never cease to teach his Occidental brother, nor ever allow himself to forget his own great spiritual maxims which have guided the course of his life for so many centuries, that "a man's life consisteth not in the things which he possesseth," and that, "except the Lord build the house, they labor in vain that build it."

When the wise men from the East and the wise men from the West join hands together and make such precepts the life centers of the social order, then we shall have true civilization in both the East and the West. Otherwise, we are not growing better; we are only going faster.